The Two Ways

The Two Ways

a commentary on the Gauri Vars *of Guru Ramdas*

AJAIB SINGH

Sant Bani Ashram, Sanbornton, New Hampshire, 1985

Commentary translated from the Punjabi by Raj Kumar Bagga and edited by Russell and Judith Perkins

Hymns of the *Gauri Vars* translated by Raj Kumar Bagga and Kent Bicknell

Calligraphy by Jerri Jo Idarius

Front cover design by Todd Smith

Back cover photo by Charlie Boynton

Photocredits: frontispiece, Jonas Gerard; p. 2, Richard Cardozo; p. 18, Tom Kuhner; pp. 36, 66, Bobbe Baker; pp. 50, 100, 136, 182, Charlie Boynton; p. 154, Neil Wolf

Library of Congress Catalog Card Number: 85-50963

International Standard Book Number: 0-89142-045-2

Blessed is the man that walketh not in the counsel of the ungodly, nor standeth in the way of sinners, nor sitteth in the seat of the scornful.
But his delight is in the law of the LORD; and in his law doth he meditate day and night.
And he shall be like a tree planted by the rivers of water, that bringeth forth his fruit in his season; his leaf also shall not wither; and whatsoever he doeth shall prosper.
The ungodly are not so: but are like the chaff which the wind driveth away.
Therefore the ungodly shall not stand in the judgment, nor sinners in the congregation of the righteous.
For the LORD knoweth the way of the righteous: but the way of the ungodly shall perish.

PSALM I

Enter ye in at the strait gate: for wide is the gate, and broad is the way, that leadeth to destruction, and many there be which go in thereat:
Because strait is the gate, and narrow is the way, which leadeth unto life, and few there be that find it.

MATTHEW 7:13-14

Out of mercy, the Satguru always takes care of the *jiva* (embodied or bound soul) and is desirous that all His disciples should have great love and faith in His feet, but the mind does not like that the jiva should attain this state. It therefore tries to draw him towards the enjoyment of sensual pleasures and wants the jiva to obey its dictates. The jivas should, therefore, continue their devotion at the feet of the Satguru, beware of the ambush of the mind and see that they do not fall into its trap.

A brief account of the ways of a *Gurumukh* and the ways of a *manmukh** is given here to enable the jiva to test and regulate his conduct. The jiva should go on applying this test to himself.

1. The dealings of the Gurumukh are always true and straight with everybody. He shuns evil and does not deceive anyone. Whatever he does, he does for the Satguru, and relies upon His mercy.

A manmukh is sly and insincere in his dealings, and will deceive others

* *Gurumukh*—"One through whom the Guru speaks," that is, one who has risen above his ego, individual mind, desires, etc., so that his higher Self which is identical with the Guru is actively manifest. *Manmukh*—"One through whom the mind speaks," that is, one who has not become a Gurumukh and is still living in the fallen state which keeps him away and separate from his higher Self, Guru or God.

to secure his own interests. He depends upon his own cleverness and intelligence, and wishes to proclaim himself.

2. A Gurumukh controls his mind and senses and is humble in spirit. He puts up with taunting words, lends a willing ear to advice and does not seek to be honored.

A manmukh does not like his mind to be curbed. He does not like to submit to anyone or obey anybody, and is jealous of the greatness of others.

3. A Gurumukh does not oppress anybody. He is always willing and ready to serve and please and wishes to do good to others. He seeks not his own fame or honor, but keeps happy and absorbed in the thoughts of the Satguru and in His Holy Feet.

A manmukh dominates others and makes them serve him. He seeks honor and does not care for others except for his own selfish interests. He enjoys being honored and made much of, and does not remain absorbed in the Holy Feet of the Satguru.

4. A Gurumukh never gives up his humility and gentleness. He does not resent it if he is slandered or slighted or shown disrespect. He regards all this as conducive to his own good.

A manmukh fears slander and dishonor, does not willingly put up with disrespect, and solicits praise.

5. A Gurumukh works hard and never remains idle.

A manmukh seeks bodily ease and comfort, and is lazy.

6. A Gurumukh leads a simple and humble life, and is ready to live contentedly on whatever falls to his lot, be it dry and unbuttered (bread), or rough and coarse (clothing).

A manmukh always loves and craves dainty dishes. He does not like to have dry and unbuttered bread and things of low value.

7. A Gurumukh is not engrossed by earthly goods and the meshes of the world, and feels no pain or pleasure in losing them or getting them. He is not upset by unbecoming remarks made against him. He keeps an eye on the salvation of his soul and on pleasing his Satguru.

A manmukh thinks too much of the world and its goods. He feels pain if he loses them and pleasure if he gets them. If one talks harshly to him, he immediately flies into anger, forgets the grace and power of the Satguru, and does not rely on Him.

8. A Gurumukh is frank and sincere in all matters. He is liberal-

minded, helps others and wishes them well. He is contented with little, and does not desire to take from others.

A manmukh is greedy. He is always ready to take things from others, but does not want to give. He always thinks of his own interest in everything and does not care for others. He goes on multiplying his desires and is not straight in his dealings.

9. A Gurumukh is not attached to worldly people. He does not crave or care for pleasures or enjoyments, nor does he long for sight-seeing and amusements. His only desire is to be at the Feet (of the Satguru), and he remains absorbed in that bliss.

A manmukh loves worldly people and things, desires enjoyment and pleasures, and feels happy in sight-seeing and amusements.

10. Whatever a Gurumukh does, he does to please his Satguru, and craves for grace and mercy from Him. He praises only the Satguru, wishes to see only Him honored, and has no worldly desires.

A manmukh has some self-interest or pleasure in whatever he does, for he cannot undertake anything which does not contribute to his self-interest. He wishes to be praised and honored, and the worldly desires predominate in him.

11. A Gurumukh is not antagonistic towards anyone; rather, he loves even those who are antagonistic to him. He is not proud of his family, caste, position or the friendship of great men; and loves devoted and spiritually minded people. He always keeps alive his love and devotion in the Feet of the Satguru, and always wishes to gain more and more the mercy and grace of the Satguru.

A manmukh is anxious to have a big family and friends, courts rich and influential people and is proud of the friendship of such persons and of his own caste. He always wishes to do things for show and cares little for the approval of the Satguru.

12. A Gurumukh is not distressed by poverty and want, but bears with fortitude any calamity that may befall him, always trusts in the mercy of the Satguru, and is grateful to Him.

A manmukh is quickly distressed by adversity and calls aloud for help. He feels pain and grumbles if he is poor.

13. A Gurumukh leaves everything to the Divine Will, and whether it turns out well or ill, he never brings in his own ego. He does not try to prove his own point nor does he try to prove the hollowness of others. He will not permit himself to be entangled in controversial acts.

Always watching the will of the Satguru, he passes his days singing the Satguru's praises.

A manmukh asserts himself in everything; for his own delight and gain, he undertakes things involving strife and dispute. He gets angry and is even ready to quarrel to maintain his own side.

14. A Gurumukh does not run after new and novel things, for he sees that they have their root in the material world. He conceals his own virtues from the world, and does not like to be praised. From whatever he sees or hears, he selects that point which is calculated to contribute to his love and devotion for the Satguru, and goes on singing the praises of the Satguru who is the treasure of all good.

A manmukh is always anxious to see and hear novel things. He is eager to pry into the secrets of others and to know their private affairs. He wishes to add to his intelligence and cleverness by gathering points from here and there, with a view to display his great intelligence and secure praise; and is highly pleased when he is praised.

15. A Gurumukh is steady in the performance of spiritual practices; always relies upon the grace and mercy of the Satguru and has unshaken faith in His Holy Feet.

A manmukh is hasty in everything and wishes to finish things hurriedly. In his haste, over and over again he forgets his trust in the grace and mercy of the Satguru and in His words.

16. All that has been said about the conduct of a Gurumukh will be acquired solely by the grace of the Satguru. Only he to whom He is merciful will receive this gift. Those who love His Holy Feet and have faith in Him will surely receive this gift one day. Love for the Holy Feet of the Satguru is the source of all virtues. All virtues will automatically come to him who receives the gift of Love; then all the manmukh characteristics will disappear in a minute.

SAR BACHAN 2:262

There are two ways—one leading to life and the other to destruction; called *Sharey Marg* and *Piray Marg*. *Piray Marg* relates to objective life and appears all beautiful and easy to follow but it results in hatred and malevolence, rigid ideology and obsessive self. The way of *Sharey Marg* lies in developing inner silence, which is harder to find. It is an uphill task and takes hard work of mind and body and purification of spirit.

When you will become broad-minded and have risen to the heights of life by sacrificing everything, you will find a vision of the Lord working in all alike, in saints and sinners, in all men and in all creation, in all birds and beasts, in all religions, in all scriptures and in all prophets.

In silence we test ourselves to find weaknesses to be weeded out. We have to wrestle with darkness and develop moral muscles and receive the message of the spirit. We must be for some time at least alone with God. When we enter more and more into silence, our desires will be eliminated, purity will be attained and the body and the mind sanctified, and we taste the Elixir of Naam Divine and know how sweet the Name is.

In silence the heart illumines; veil after veil is removed. In the heart shineth the Light, and the very silence becomes vocal giving vent to the Music of the Spheres reverberating in all creation. When the Light is seen shining within your heart and the Music of the Spheres becomes audible, you behold the Light in all, that is, outside you see the One Light in all. This is the universal vision that the One is in all and all are in One. Blessed is he, the man of Illumination, for wherever he be, he dwelleth with the One Eternal.

Such a blessed one belongeth not to this color or caste or creed; he belongeth to all. The great mystic Rumi says:

I am neither Christian nor Jew,
Neither Gaber nor Turk,
I am not of the East; I am not of the West;
I am not of the land; Not of the sea;
I belong to the soul of the Beloved,
I have seen that the two are One.
And One I see, and One I know.
One I see, and One I adore.
He is the First, and He is the Last;
He is the outward, and He is the inward too.

This is the ultimate goal before each one of you. I wish all who care to achieve this goal. All feasible help of the Master will be at hand.

SANT KIRPAL SINGH JI
April 2, 1967

Table of Contents

The Two Ways

The Satguru is the Gracious One in Whose eyes
everyone is equal.
He looks at everyone equally, but each receives
according to his receptivity.
In the Satguru lies the Nectar and the highest
status of the Lord.
Nanak says, "By Grace one meditates on the Lord;
Rare Gurumukhs obtain Him.
Egoism and maya - both are poison.
People lose continuously in this world.
Profits lie in the wealth of the Lord, which is
acquired by meditation on the Shabd of the
Gurumukhs.
The filth and poison of egoism are removed by
keeping the Nectar of the Lord in the heart.
Those Gurumukhs on whom the Lord showers
His grace, accomplish all Their works.
Nanak says, Those who meet the Ones who are
already united with Him meet the Creator.
O Lord, You are the True Lord and You are True.
All remember You and all cling to Your Feet.
Your praise is beautiful;
You take the ones who praise You across.
Gurumukhs get the fruit;
They remain absorbed in the True Naam.
My Lord, You are great and great is Your glory.

All the praise and talk is tasteless without the meditation of Naam.
Manmukhs praise their egoism and fight because of attachment and ego.
Those whom they praise, die;
And those who criticize also die.
Nanak says, Gurumukhs get liberation by meditating on the Lord and His Supreme Sound.
O Satguru, show me the Naam of the Lord so I may meditate on Him within my mind.
Nanak says, The Naam of the Lord is pure.
By repeating it one removes all pain.
You yourself are Nirankar (the Formless One) and Niranjan (unaffected by maya).
Those who meditate on You single-mindedly lose all their pains.
There is no equal to You,
To whom one may tell his pains.
O Lord, You Yourself are the giver;
You are unaffected by Maya;
You are the Truth;
And You are pleasing to me.
You are my True Lord, and Your Naam is also True.

1

The Two Ways

This is the *bani* or the writing of Guru Ramdas Ji, the fourth Guru of the Sikhs. In this bani, he will tell us how the great souls come into this world to liberate us other souls, and how, when They do that job, They are opposed and harassed by the people, and what happens to the people who crucify the Saints and give Them a hard time: how they, after having done this bad deed, try to justify themselves and convince people that they are still true; how they proclaim this "truth" after they have done this very bad deed: and what happens to them after they leave the world.

In this bani, Guru Ramdas Ji will tell us who comes to the Path of the Masters and how they come; how the souls are deluded by the Negative Power even after coming to the Path; how those souls who obey their minds leave the Path; and how the Master Power again brings them onto the Path.

Further, He will tell us the difference between the *manmukhs* and the *gurumukhs* ["those through whom the mind speaks" and "those through whom the Guru speaks," respectively]. He will tell us what their qualities are and what happens to them when they leave the world. All this means that many aspects of the Path of the Masters will be covered in these two weeks that I'm here [at Sant Bani Ashram], and later, I hope that these talks will be available to you on tapes, or maybe they will eventually be published in the magazine or as a book; and then you will know a lot about the Path which you have not known up until now.

Those who think that now we are on the Path and have been initiated, so we can do anything we want—we can do any bad deed we want, we can criticize anybody—they should listen to this bani very carefully, and pay attention to it: because it is a law of nature that whatever bad deed you do, you will definitely be punished for it. Master Sawan Singh Ji always said that the Negative Power gives no concession: every karma, good or bad, whatever you have done, that has to be paid off. You have to suffer or enjoy the reaction of that karma. Either the disciple has to pay off the bad karma, or the Master has to do it; but every single karma will have to be paid or the Negative Power will not let you go.

During this time of two weeks, you will even learn from this bani that nobody can become a Saint overnight. If one is to become a Saint, he has to work very hard; he has to meditate. If he has become a Saint by meditation, His power and His competence will not decrease; and if some people form a party and say that he is a Saint, and if in fact he is not, if he has not done the meditation, he does not become a Saint in that way. Nobody can become a Saint just because he has the support of a few people. The great souls Who come in this world work very hard, give a lot of pain to Their body, and keep themselves involved in Bhajan and Simran day and night; and only then can they achieve this high status and become Saints. They do all these things because They have to demonstrate to other people, and make them do the things which They have done. Unless one has done something, He cannot make other people do it.

Masters do not generally criticize anyone in the satsang, and moreover, They do not personally criticize anyone. And They never allow any of their disciples to criticize others, because They want to keep Their lives pure and they want their disciples to keep their lives pure; because by criticism we carry the dirt of others.

In His old age Guru Amardas Ji served His Master, Guru Angad Dev, very much. He was so humble that after Guru Angad Dev left the body and He started doing Satsang, Datu and Dasu, sons of Guru Angad Dev, came; and when they saw that Guru Amardas was doing Satsang, they were very upset and kicked Him off the dais, saying, "You used to be the servant of our house, and now you have become the owner of the throne of our Father. How is that possible?"

When Guru Amardas was kicked off the dais, He didn't get upset with them. Instead He started massaging their legs, and He said, "Forgive me, because I have this old bony body, and I am afraid that because of these bones, you might have hurt yourself when you kicked me." He was so humble that he didn't get upset at them: instead he said to them, "Take this dais, you sit on this, I don't have to do anything with this *gaddi,* this throne." And Guru Amardas left that place quietly, taking his mattresses and his few possessions. On his way, He was robbed by some thieves, and he became a homeless person. Eventually he came to Goindwal, a place in Punjab. The chief of that village was a shepherd by profession named Gondar. He didn't recognize Guru

Amardas; he was following the sons of Guru Angad Dev, so he started opposing and criticizing Guru Amardas.

Despite the criticism at Goindwal, Guru Amardas started His satsang there. But you know that the Satsang of the Perfect Master is such that if anyone comes there to see Them with full love and faith in Them, and if they are very receptive, they always become of the Masters. So whenever anybody went to the Satsang of Guru Amardas, he would appreciate Him and become His disciple. But in that village there lived a yogi who used to perform austerities. Before Guru Amardas came there and started His satsang, people used to come to him, but after Guru Amardas came, not many were left with the yogi, and he became very jealous of Guru Amardas. So he joined with Gondar, the chief of the village, and he told Gondar, "There should be some way to throw Guru Amardas out of here."

Once there was a drought in the area. People were very worried; all the crops were dependent on the rain. So they came to Guru Amardas and requested Him to shower some grace on them. Guru Amardas replied, "It is all in the Will of God. Let us see what is in His Will. If He wants us to have rain and to have a good crop, we will definitely have it." But that was not enough for the illiterate farmers. So that yogi took advantage of the situation: he told Gondar, the shepherd who was chief of that village, "If Guru Amardas is thrown out of here, then this area will have rain. Guru Amardas is an atheist; he doesn't believe in the existence of gods and goddesses. How can we get rain when we have such an atheist in our area? If you want to have the rain, you should throw out this Amardas."

Illiterate farmers do not think of the future; they just do whatever they are told to. So they were misled by that yogi, and they threw out Guru Amardas from the village. But still there was no rain.

Later on, Bhai Jetha, a disciple of Guru Amardas, came there, searching for the Guru. Somehow he knew that he had been living in Goindwal but when he came, he didn't find Him there. He was very worried, and asked people, "Where is my Master?" They replied that he was thrown out of the village because with his presence there was no rain in this area, and they were told by the yogi that if they threw him out, they would get some rain. So Bhai Jetha said, "Did you get any rain after you threw my Master out?" They replied, "No, we didn't get any rain."

Bhai Jetha was a great meditator and he possessed many supernatural powers. He thought of taking revenge and teaching a great lesson to that yogi. So using his supernatural powers, he told the farmers, "This yogi is so blessed and precious, that if you will take him to your fields, wherever he will step, wherever he will take his body, in that part of the village, you will have rain." So everybody wanted that yogi to visit their field so that they may have the rain. And it worked; they took the yogi from field to field because they all wanted the rain very badly. And the time came when everybody wanted the yogi to visit their field. And in that way he was chased, pulled and pushed; he was so much pulled and pushed that he died on the spot.

Eventually Bhai Jetha found the place where Guru Amardas was living; the Guru, after leaving Goindwal had made a hut in the wilderness. He had closed the hut, and was sitting inside. Because the Masters, those who have done meditation, when They see that the people are not receptive to Them and they don't want to take advantage of Their presence in this world, They just go away from the world. They have nothing to do with the world, They aren't attached to the world, and They have no interest in the world. They have come into this world only to give out the Message of God; and if the people don't want to accept it, then what is the point of Their living in the world?

So thinking that, Guru Amardas went away in the wilderness and He didn't want to see anyone. He put a sign on the front door of the hut: "Nobody should come through this door." So when Bhai Jetha, Baba Budha, and Bhai Gurdas, all devoted disciples, came to that place, they were very surprised to see this sign. But they said, "Master has told us not to open this door; but we can break down the rear wall!" So they broke through the rear wall, and in that way they had the darshan of their Master. But Guru Amardas was displeased with Bhai Jetha, because he had used supernatural power to teach a lesson to that yogi. He didn't give him His darshan; He turned his back on Bhai Jetha. And Bhai Jetha was so sorry that he said, "Master, why are you displeased with me?" Guru Amardas replied, "Listen, I didn't tell you to use your supernatural powers to defeat those who are opposing me. We have to live in the will of God, and we are not supposed to do that. Why did you do it? Why did you go against my teachings? I didn't tell you to convince people that I am the Real One. Why did you do it?" So Bhai Jetha apologized. And then they all cooperated and helped Guru Amardas very much, because after that, He started giving Initiation and holding Satsang.

This particular bani on which I am going to comment now was written by Guru Ramdas, the fourth Guru, Who was the successor to Guru Amardas. In this bani, he will show us exactly what happened to Guru Amardas and how things went when He was opposed. Despite the criticism of the people, and their opposition, He still worked. He gave the secret of the Naam, and He gave Initiation to the people.

The Negative Power received many boons when this creation was created. One of the boons was that whenever Perfect Masters come into this world, They should not be allowed to perform miracles to attract people. That is why, when Masters come,They do not perform any miracles. It is not a big thing for Them to give an eye to a blind man, or a leg to a crippled man: They can do it very easily; it is just play for Them. But They are not allowed to do that. If They were allowed to do it, just one Perfect Master would have been enough to liberate the whole creation.

Another boon which the Negative Power asked for and got from Sat Purush, is that wherever souls get birth, they should be content with it and not complain. They may try for better, but they should not complain, and they should be pleased with whatever they have been given. So you know that the body of a pig is very difficult to live in; he has to eat dirt, he is always dirty, he is not comfortable at all. But still he is very contented and happy in the body which he has been given. He never complains; not even pigs want to die. If you try to kill them, they will scream and resist.

The third boon was, wherever the souls are born, they should not have any knowledge of their past. They should not know what bad karma they are suffering from, and what good karma they are enjoying.

These are the boons which the Negative Power received, and this is why Masters never attract disciples by performing miracles. But you know that even if the perfume seller doesn't want to sell his perfume, sometimes it happens that his bottle is left open; and in that way people know who is selling perfumes, and they come to him by themselves. In the same way, even though Masters do not perform any miracles, those who are receptive to the grace of the Master, and those who have an open heart for Him, they recognize the perfection of the Master somehow. That is why they come to the Path of the Masters. But Masters never perform any miracles: They never curse anybody, and They never prophesy that "You will have this" or "you will not have this." They are not allowed to do that. Even though they are able to do this without any problem—it is very easy for them—still, They are not allowed, so They don't.

The Satguru is the Gracious One in Whose eyes everyone is equal.

Now Guru Ramdas Ji says, Whenever God wants to liberate us, He puts His power, His skill, His competence, within some human pole; and using that human pole, He liberates us and gives us good teachings. If He tried to do that through the animals and other lower creatures, we would never have been able to take advantage of that. Because we are human, He keeps His power, His skill, within some human form. On one side Master is connected with God, and on the other side He is connected with the world. He is the only person who brings the message of God and gives it to us.

But for Him everybody is equal. He looks at His Sangat with the same eyes, or with the same sight, as He does His physical children; for Him the foe and friend are equal; He has an equal angle of vision for everybody. By meditating, He has reached up to this point: He can see God working in every leaf, and in every creature in this creation. That is why He sees God functioning everywhere. He has complete knowledge of how God is absorbed and is present at every place, and how he has to see God working within everyone. When our soul rises above the level of mind and the organs of senses, and when we look from above to the world below, then we can easily see that God is working everywhere. When we rise high enough to see the world below working, then we can easily see God functioning everywhere; and then we can say that God is living, or God is present, in every leaf, every creature, in the friend and in the enemy God lives.

When we look at things from below—from the level of the mind and the organs of senses, then we see different faces; we see different people. That is why we say, "One is good, one is bad"; and that is why we discriminate between people and find differences in them.

Guru Sahib says, "As long as one is involved in duality, he says 'good' and 'bad.' But Gurumukhs have become one, they have absorbed Themselves in the Ultimate One, in God, and that is why They see Him working everywhere."

He looks at everyone equally, but each receives according to his receptivity.

Master looks at us with the same sight. His feelings towards us are equal; for everyone it is alike and He has the same amount of Grace for everybody. But we receive from Him according to our receptivity. The more receptive we are towards Him, the more Grace we will feel; and the less receptive we are, the less we will feel. It is like a father who has two sons: One son obeys him, takes his advice to heart, goes to school, and obeys the teachers and the masters there; and in that way he awakens the power of knowledge which he has within himself. Whereas the other son does not obey his father; he doesn't go to school, he doesn't obey his teachers; and therefore he doesn't do anything to awaken his sleeping knowledge. When both of them become older, the one who obeyed his teachers and his father, becomes a good, respected man in the world; whereas the other one, because he is illiterate, doesn't get a respectable job or any respect in the world. But still they are the sons of the same father; the affection, the love and the attention of the father was the same for both of them; but because their receptivity was different—one was obeying his father, the other was not—their future was different.

In the same way, in the Path of the Masters, no doubt we all are the children of God. But if we don't obey the Master, if we don't do what He wants us to do, then our condition is like that boy who was not able to get a respectable job. That is why, in the Path of the Masters, there are both *gurumukhs* and *manmukhs*—the gurumukhs are those who obey the Masters, and the manmukhs are the ones who don't obey the Masters, who may not even come to the Path. We are still the children of the same God, but there is no way that gurumukhs and manmukhs can be called similar or the same, even though they are children of the same God. Guru Ramdas says that in the Path of the Masters, gurumukhs and manmukhs are like water and oil—they can't mix—they will always remain different. Their qualities are different, everything is different. Again, a father has two sons; one passes his examination, the other fails. The Gurumukhs liberate the souls, whereas the manmukhs take the souls in the other direction, and keep them in this world.

In the Satguru lies the Nectar and the highest status of the Lord.

Sant Satgurus have worked very hard and after meditating very completely They have manifested the Naam within Them. They have spent a major portion of Their life in this direction. Because of Their constant hard work, They have been able to manifest Naam. That is why that Naam is compared with nectar: because it is not an easy thing to manifest it within ourselves.

It is the only thing which is worth receiving, or asking for, from the Master: the wealth of the devotion of Naam which He has collected and which He has manifested. This is the only thing which will go with us; it is such a thing which will never be destroyed, which can never be stolen by anyone; and it is the only thing which helps us in this world, as well as in the world beyond. As long as the Masters live in the physical body, They do not say, "You take me as your Master." They say, "Your Master is within you. That is the Form of the Shabda, that Naam which is manifested here." They don't attach Their disciples to Their body. They connect the disciples with the Shabda which is working and which is manifested within them. The body of the Master is not going to exist forever in this world; neither is the body of the disciple. The form of the disciple is the soul, or *Surat,* and the form of the Master is the Shabd. Even if the Master leaves the body right after initiating the soul, that disciple does not need to go to any other Master, because his Master is still within him. The only difference that the departure of the physical body of the Master makes is, that the disciples of that Master are no longer benefitted by the physical darshan of the Master. Such dear ones, whose Master has left the physical body, can go to the Satsang of their Master's successor; and if they have any questions to ask, they can ask them of Him; and if they have any obstacles, any hindrance in their meditation, they can request Him to help them; and in that way they can get the benefit of the living Master.

The Master who has left the body cannot come back and initiate the new souls. Only the new Master, the living Master, can initiate new souls.

Nanak says, "By Grace one meditates on the Lord;
Rare Gurumukhs obtain Him."

We go in the company of the Master only when God showers Grace on us. And we get connected with Shabd Naam only if Master showers grace on us.

Egoism and maya—both are poison.
People lose continuously in this world.

Egoism is the great big wall or obstacle between us and God. As for maya—nobody has ever been contented with maya. Even if we get the wealth of the whole world, still we are not contented; there is no peace or happiness in collecting the maya of the world. Maya never stays at one place forever; it is not permanent; it goes on changing. It is like the shadow of the tree which is at one place in the morning, in the afternoon at another place, and in the evening at another; and then there comes a time when the shadow is gone. So that is why the Masters say, there is no peace or happiness in collecting maya. Even if God gives us the wealth of the whole world, still we will not be contented. Guru Nanak says, "Even if you collect the wealth of the whole world, still your hunger will not be satisfied."

Profits lie in the wealth of the Lord, which is acquired by meditation on the Shabd of the Gurumukhs.

Gurumukhs meditate on Shabd Naam on this physical plane, and when they go, they take nothing but the wealth of Shabd Naam with them. And they make their disciples meditate only on Shabd Naam.

The filth and poison of egoism are removed by keeping the Nectar of the Lord in the heart.

Why do we have to do the meditation of Shabd Naam? Because the valley—the obstacle, the hindrance of egoism—which is between us and God, can be crossed only by doing the meditation of Shabd Naam. That is why it is very important, if any one wants to realize God and reach Him, to first of all remove this wall of egoism.

Those Gurumukhs on whom the Lord showers His grace, accomplish all Their works.

Doing the meditation of Shabd Naam does not give us any defect in our body; nor does it make us lose in our worldly business. Instead of losing, we gain a lot if we are meditating. It helps us make progress in our worldly business also. Whatever work we start, if we do meditation before it, definitely we will have good results and we will become successful in it. So it is very important; even to get worldly success, if we meditate, it helps.

Nanak says, Those who meet the Ones who are already united with Him meet the Creator.

Only those who have come in the selection of God from the very beginning, come and take the gift of Shabd Naam; only they remain in touch with the Shabd Naam; only they meditate on it.

O Lord, You are the True Lord and You are True.

Now Guru Ramdas Ji says, "O Lord, You are True." "True" means that which never perishes, is never destroyed, and which is existing from the very beginning. He says, "You existed even before this creation was created, You will exist after it also, You exist even now. You are the Giver to everybody and You are the Lord, the Master, of everyone."

All remember You; and all cling to Your Feet.

Now He says, "Those who appreciate You, sing Your praise, and do

Your devotion, they are good. Those who do all this, reach their Home." Even the animals and birds express their gratitude and thank God in their own way and in their own language. Farid Sahib says, "I sacrifice myself on those birds who live on the branches of the trees in the forest, and who go and search for food on the ground, and who suffer so much, but still do not give up the hope of God, nor forget God."

We know that the birds wake up early in the morning, before we do, and they start singing the praise of God in their own language and in their own voice.

On the other hand, a man has been given many comfortable things. But even if he eats many good things, when he has to get up in the morning to do his devotion, he makes excuses. He says, "My body is not feeling good. I have pain in my knees, . . . " etc. He finds many excuses for not doing the meditation. So Farid Sahib says, "Even the birds, those who get up early in the morning and remember the Name of the Lord, they are better than those men who don't get up in the morning to sit in the remembrance of God."

Your praise is beautiful;
You take the ones who praise You across.

Now he says, "O Satguru, O Lord, Your glory is very beautiful, and those who appreciate You, who sing Your glory, Your praise, they never remain in this world; they become detached from this world, and get liberated."

Mahatmas tell us that we can sing the praise of the Master and appreciate Him, only if we have love for Him. But we don't have enough love for Him, so instead of appreciating His existence in this world, we appreciate the existence of the worldly things; because we are in love with the worldly things.

Gurumukhs get the fruit;
They remain absorbed in the True Naam.

Gurumukhs appreciate and sing the praise of the Master always. Whether they are asleep or awake, whether it is day or night, no matter what they are doing, they continuously sing the songs of praise of the Master. And what do they get from God? What is the reward that God gives them? God loves them; God embraces them; God welcomes them to His Home, and God honors them. That is what they get from God when they appreciate Him.

My Lord, You are great and great is Your glory.

"You are the donor and giver of life to everybody; You give to everybody in this world; that is why Your glory is great. And those who sing Your praise, those who sing Your glory, they also become great."

All the praise and talk is tasteless without the meditation of Naam.

Whatever appreciation we have for the worldly things, no matter what we praise in this world, we do not get any taste of it. If we do not praise the Master, if we do not sing the praise and the glory of meditation, if we do not involve ourselves in that, we do not get any taste from worldly things, because they are tasteless.

Manmukhs praise their egoism and fight because of attachment and ego.

Even if manmukhs come to the Path, because their egoism is very strong, whatever they do in the Path, is also full of egoism; they follow the Path only to feed their ego.

Master Sawan Singh Ji used to say, "All that you have done becomes undone when egoism comes." He used to say, "You may do a lot of work, of good things, but then if you have the feeling of egoism—if we say, 'we have done this'—it is as if we had put some ashes all over delicious food."

Those whom they praise, die;
And those who criticize also die.

Manmukhs are involved in praising the world and worldly things. They say, "I have done this, I have done that." And, "That relative is very good; he has a great post," etc. But what is going to happen in the end? All the relatives and everything are going to be left here, and nobody will go with us. So what is the use of appreciating and singing the praise of those who are not going to go with us?

Nanak says, Gurumukhs get liberation by meditating on the Lord and His Supreme Sound.

What do Gurumukhs do? They do the devotion of Naam, they sing the praise of Naam, they praise and appreciate Master. Because they sing the glory of Naam and meditate on it, they easily get liberated from this world.

O Satguru, show me the Naam of the Lord so I may meditate on Him within my mind.

Satguru comes onto this physical plane to tell us, "Do the meditation of Shabd Naam because your soul is thirsty from ages and ages, and if you will do that meditation she will get satisfied and become alive again."

Nanak says, The Naam of the Lord is pure.
By repeating it one removes all pain.

Masters tell us that Naam is very holy, and those who meditate on it, and within whom Naam is manifested, they also become very holy. Naam is not just a few words; Naam is the attention of the Master; Naam is the power of the Master. He within whom it is manifested, becomes holy; moreover, he within whom Master puts his Naam also becomes holy. That is why Kabir Sahib says, "Even the leper whose body oozes dirt and blood, and who smells bad—if he is doing the meditation of Naam, he is much better than someone with a body made of gold but who is not doing the meditation of Naam."

You yourself are Nirankar (the Formless One) and Niranjan (unaffected by maya).
Those who meditate on You single-mindedly lose all their pains.

Now Guru Ramdas Ji sings the praise of the Lord. He says, "You are unaffected by Maya, and You are above everything in the world, and those who do your devotion also rise above all this, they become free from the pain of birth and death, and they get liberated."

There is no equal to You,
To whom one may tell his pains.

Now the Master says, "O Lord, You have no equal that we may go to and tell about our pains and sorrows, instead of coming to You. So it is better for us to come and kneel before You and tell You about our pain."

O Lord, You Yourself are the giver;
You are unaffected by Maya;

You are the Truth; and You are pleasing to me.
You are my True Lord, and Your Naam is also True.

Now He says, "O Lord, You are the giver, and You create the yearning within the souls to come to the Master; You inspire them from within. You Yourself bring them to the Feet of the Master. Distance makes no difference to him who is being inspired by You and pulled by You." That is why the disciple may be living millions of miles away from the Master, but if he has been inspired by God, he will come to the Master. Many times it happens that those who are not inspired by God, who have not been chosen by God, even if they are living close to the Master, do not take any advantage of it. That is why He says, "You are the Giver. When You give such a gift to someone, You never repent."

Within the mind is the disease of egoism.
The rascal manmukhs are lost in the illusion.
Nanak says, Get free of this disease by
meeting with Sadhus and Satgurus.
The mind and body of the Gurumukhs are
absorbed in the love of the Lord.
Nanak says, I take refuge in You, O Lord.
Make me unite with You with the grace of
the Guru.
You are the Creator, the Unreachable Being.
With whom should we compare You?
If there were someone like You we would have
said so.
You alone are like Yourself.
You are present within everyone;
But only Gurumukhs can realize You.
You are the True Lord of all and are higher
than all.
Whatever You do happens - Why should we
grieve?
I have love for my Beloved in my mind and
body during all eight watches of the day.
Nanak says, O Lord, shower grace so that
meeting the Satguru I may live in happiness.
In whose heart their is love for the Beloved,
Whatever they speak is pleasing.
Nanak says, God Himself knows whom He
has blessed with love for the Beloved.

You are the Creator. You are unerring, and are not subject to any error.
O True One, whatever you do is good. One understands this only when the Master makes one understand through Shabd.
You are all-in-all and are capable of doing everything.
There is no one like You.
You are the unreachable Gracious Lord. All meditate upon you.
All the souls are yours and you are the owner of them and you are the only liberator.
Listen, O Dear One, to the message of love, hearing which the eyes are attentively fixed on the Lord.
Nanak says, Those who are united with the Beloved by the Master live in happiness.
Satguru is the gracious giver who always showers Grace.
Satguru is without enmity from within as He sees only One Lord within all.
Those who keep enmity toward Him who is without enmity are never happy.
Satguru wishes good for all. Why should bad things come to Him ?
Nanak says, The Creator knows everything-nothing is hidden from Him.

He whom the Lord makes great is considered the Great One.
God forgives those with whom He is pleased, and they are liked by Him.
If anyone competes with Him he is an ignorant fool.
He whom the Master unites with Himself sings the Master's praise,
Nanak says, He who has understood and is absorbed in the True One is perfectly true.
God is true, unaffected by Maya; the immortal One
Without any fear, without any enmity and formless.
Those who meditate on Him with one mind and one heart
Lose their burden of egoism.
Praise to the Gurumukhs and the Saints who have meditated on the Lord.
If one criticizes the Perfect Satguru, the whole world curses him.
The Lord Himself resides in the Satguru and He Himself is the Protector.
Blessed are the ones who sing the praises of the Master. I salute them.
Nanak says, I sacrifice myself to those who meditate on the Creator.

He Himself created the earth; He Himself created the sky,
He created the creatures and He Himself feeds them.
He Himself resides in everyone; He Himself is the abode of qualities.
Nanak says, Meditate on Naam so that all the sins may be cut.
You, the True Lord, are the Truth; the Truth is pleasing to You, the True One.
Those who praise You, the True One, the servants of Yama do not come near them.
Those within whose heart the True Lord is pleasing
Have bright faces in the court of the Lord.
The false ones are thrown back.
Those in whose hearts there is falsehood and deception,
They always get pain.
The faces of the false ones become black,
And the false ones become unreal.

2

To Face the Tiger

Within the mind is the disease of egoism.
The rascal manmukhs are lost in the illusion.

We know that if we are sick we cannot do any work in the world. If the body is not fit, how can we? In the same way when our mind is sick, we cannot get ourselves connected with Shabd Naam, or meditate properly. What are the diseases which our mind has? Lust, anger, greed, attachment, and egoism—these are the sicknesses by which our mind is affected.

We can serve our Master only when we have a pure mind, because a pure mind doesn't take us away from the service of the Master.

When we connect our soul with Shabd, after completing our Simran, and crossing the stars, moon and sun, when the form of the Master is manifested—reaching that place then "I and mine" go away.

When the I-hood disappears and only "Thou" is there, then the duty of the disciple ends and the duty of the Master starts. After that, Master takes the soul from one plane to another until he finally reaches his Home.

We can do only one work at a time. Either we can do the meditation of Shabd Naam, or we can enjoy wordly pleasures. Where there is lust, Naam cannot be manifested there; where the Naam has been manifested, at that place lust never comes. A man who has manifested Naam within him is not bothered by lust.

Kabir Sahib has compared lust and Naam with night and day. He says that as night and day do not exist at the same time and in the same place, so lust and Naam do not manifest at the same time in the same place.

So Guru Ramdas Ji says that you have this disease within you, and if you want to remove it, you should go to the Perfect Master.

Now this question may arise: you may say that you do go into the company of the Master always, but still this power of lust has not decreased within you and you have not become free from it. There is no doubt that you come to Satsang and that you have love for the Master also, but your condition is just like a stone in the water. No matter how long you go on pouring water on a stone, it will not absorb a single drop; even after a year, the stone will remain dry.

In the same way, no doubt you come to the Satsang, have love for the Master, listen to Him; but the things which are talked about there and which you are expected to do, and are told to do, you don't do them. And that is why this energy of lust doesn't decrease in you.

Masters explain to us that no matter how much wood you go on putting in the fire, it will never be extinguished in that way. The more you feed the fire the more it will grow. In the same way, if you think, "Let us enjoy lust today, and tomorrow it will stop," that is not possible. The more you enjoy lust, the more desire for enjoying it will come.

So Guru Ramdas Ji says, "O Nanak, if you want to remove this disease, go in the company of the Gurumukhs and do what they tell you to do." If you want to remove the sickness of mind, after going in the company of the Master, do meditation as much as possible; only then will you be able to purify your soul.

Nanak says, Get free of this disease by meeting with Sadhus and Satgurus.
The mind and body of the Gurumukhs are absorbed in the love of the Lord.

What is there in the meditation of Shabd Naam? By doing the meditation of Shabd Naam, when we reach Trikuti and the limits of Brahm, we leave our mind there. Once we have taken our mind to its original home, after that when we come back, our mind who has been behaving like an enemy to us starts behaving like a friend. Instead of retarding our progress, he helps us in progressing more.

Nanak says, I take refuge in You, O Lord.
Make me unite with You with the grace of the Guru.

Guru Ramdas Ji Maharaj says, "I lay myself down in front of my Master, I sacrifice myself for the Master, because great is my Master who saved me from this disease."

You are the Creator, the Unreachable Being.
With whom should we compare You?

If there were someone like You we would have said so.
You alone are like Yourself.

Now Guru Ramdas Ji sings the praise of the Lord. He says, "O Lord, You are the greatest of all. There is no one to whom we can compare You. You are Almighty. You are the Giver, the Protector for everyone."

Kabir Sahib says, "If you ask a dumb man to describe the taste of rock candy, how can he do it? All he can do is show how happy he is. In the same way when you have realized God, if someone asks you what God is like, how can you express it? He cannot be contained in any expression. All you can do is show how happy you are if you have realized Him."

Master Sawan Singh Ji often used to say that if you want to describe the beauty of Taj Mahal, the famous building built by Emperor Shah Jahan in India, by comparing it to any other building we cannot do that: there is no building in this world to which we can compare the Taj Mahal. So if we cannot even compare the Taj Mahal to any other building in this world, how can we describe the beauty of God? How can we say that anything is like God? God is unique and His beauty cannot be described. It is better to concentrate and go within and see the beauty of God for ourselves.

You are present within everyone;
But only Gurumukhs can realize You.
You are the True Lord of all and are higher than all.
Whatever You do happens—Why should we grieve?

Guru Sahib says, "O Lord, there is not even one place where You do not reside. You reside in everybody, even in the bodies of animals and birds, and everywhere. There is no place without Your presence in this world. But within whom do You get manifested? You manifest Yourself only within the Gurumukhs"—because Gurumukhs have manifested God within them. That is why they see God functioning everywhere, and why they come into the world with the message of God. They tell us that God resides within everybody—within you, and us—and that is why Gurumukhs say that we should always see God working in everyone. They say this because they have manifested God within them. So here Guru Sahib says, "There is no place in this world where You are not present. You are present everywhere."

Mahatmas tell us that there are two types of people who live in this world: the Gurumukhs and the manmukhs. Gurumukhs are those who have manifested God within them, who see God everywhere. The manmukhs have not manifested God within them, they do not believe in the existence of God, and say that God does not reside in everyone.

So Guru Ramdas Ji in a way is putting a question to us. He says, "God made man of five elements; if anyone wants to be equal to God let him try making the man with four elements, or even with three elements."

In the field of medicine, people have progressed a lot. They have even performed things which seem miraculous: they have invented many medicines and devices by which they have eased the pain and the sufferings of the bodies. But when the time of death comes, no doctor has been successful in finding the place where the soul comes out of the body, or where it goes after it leaves. And nobody has ever succeeded in postponing death even for a moment.

Kabir Sahib says that the doctor gives the medicine but the soul is not in his control, because that belongs to God and whenever God wants it He can take it.

I have love for my Beloved in my mind and body during all the eight watches of the day.
Nanak says, O Lord, shower grace so that meeting the Satguru I may live in happiness.

Now He says, "I have manifested God within me and twenty-four hours a day I have unbreakable, constant love for God within. But by whose Grace have I been able to do all this? It is by the grace of my Master, my Satguru, that I have been able to have constant love for God."

In whose heart there is love for the Beloved, Whatever they speak is pleasing.
Nanak says, God Himself knows whom He has blessed with love for the Beloved.

Within whom is God manifested? God is love, and when that love is manifested, that person is always liked by others, and God also adores him; God likes whatever he does; because God likes the innocent people and God knows those within whom He is manifested.

Masters make us understand that if God could be realized by bathing in holy waters, the frogs and fishes who live in that water would have realized God before us. If God could be achieved by cleverness, the innocent people would never have had the chance to realize Him. God is such a thing which cannot be bought. If He could be bought by material wealth, then only the rich people would have got Him; the poor people would have found no place before Him.

Bulleh Shah says: "O Mullah (priest) now you stop reading and quoting from the books. Tell me something of love."

He was the same Bulleh Shah who was very learned, and had been a priest in the mosque of Lahore. And yet he uttered those words.

When he came to Inayat Shah and got Kalma or Naam-initiation from Him, he asked his Master, "Because I have this job of priest of the mosque, if I stop doing all the things I am doing there, then people will say I have become an atheist; what should I do?" Inayat Shah told him: "Bulleh Shah, I don't tell you to stop doing those things, but now that you have got this Kalma, you should meditate upon it. And after meditating, if you see that the things which you are doing now are better than what you have been given, then you can continue doing them. I won't say that you should stop." So, when Bulleh Shah went back to his job and meditated also, and he realized the greatness and glory of the Master, he stopped doing all the rites and rituals. When he went to see his Master again, Inayat Shah asked him, "Do you still go to the mosque and do all the rites and rituals and make prayers there?" Bulleh Shah answered, "Master, now what can I do? Should I make the prayers or should I look at You? I have forgotten even the name of the Kaaba, I have even forgotten that I am supposed to go to the mosque; because wherever I look, I see only You."

You are the Creator. You are unerring, and are not subject to any error.
O True One, whatever You do is good. One understands this only when the Master makes one understand through Shabd.

"O Lord, You never forget anything. You have created this creation and every soul and You never forget any of them. Whatever is happening in this world, whatever You are doing in this creation, that can be realized only by the Gurumukhs."

You are all-in-all and are capable of doing everything.
There is no one like You.
You are the unreachable Gracious Lord. All meditate upon you.
All the souls are yours and you are the owner of them and you are the only liberator.

Now he says: "You belong to everyone, and you are Gracious. And those who meditate upon Your Name and those who remember You and do Your devotion, You forgive them, You liberate them, and You cut the attachments of the world for them, and You remove the bindings of the Angels of Death, if You are gracious on them, You can remove those bonds and liberate them."

He says that the devotion of the Lord is the giver of happiness and the remover of sins. It is like Nectar. The devotion of the Lord is the remover of lust, anger, and other passions.

Those who search for God lovingly and have faith, they definitely reach God. But we cannot realize God by our own efforts. We can realize God only after meeting the Masters and only by having Their guidance.

Listen, O Dear One, to the message of love, hearing which the eyes are attentively fixed on the Lord.
Nanak says, Those who are united with the Beloved by the Master live in happiness.

When we heard about such a God and got the message of God, we broke into tears of remorse that we didn't remember such a God. And at once the Name of God came on our lips, and day and night now we are in the remembrance of God.

Master used to say that the coming of the loving soul to the Master is just like bringing the dry gunpowder in contact with fire. If the gunpowder is damp, it takes some time to make it dry, and after that it catches fire.

In the Way of the Saints it is not necessary for anyone to be initated for twenty years or fifty years before his soul is withdrawn from the body. It all depends on the efforts of the dear one. Only by his efforts he can withdraw the soul from the body as soon as he wants. It all depends on his efforts because the grace of the Master is equal and it is always there.

Those who stay up in the night and work hard, always become successful. Kabir says, "Happy is all the world who eat and sleep. But unhappy is Kabir who stays up and weeps."

Satguru is the gracious giver who always showers Grace.
Satguru is without enmity from within as He sees only One Lord within all.

Now he says that Satguru comes into this world as the gracious One, and He knows only to shower grace on everyone. He has no enmity towards anyone; He is without enmity.

You may read the history of the Masters and you will find how people harassed and troubled the Master but Masters never cursed them.

When Guru Arjan Dev was made to sit on the hot pan and when the hot, burning sand was put on His head, at that time Mian Mir, one of his devotees who was very devoted to Him and was very loving, came there and he felt terrible because such a bad thing was happening there. And he requested Guru Arjan Dev, "O Lord, if You allow me I can raze the city of Lahore to the ground. If You allow me I can do anything." Guru Arjan replied: "Mian Mir, I can do that also, but this is the Will of God and I want to remain in the Will of God. I like the Will of God, it is very sweet." He said, "O Lord, Your Will is very sweet, and Nanak always asks for the boon of Naam."

When Mansur's hands were cut and his eyes were taken out, still he said: "O Lord, have mercy on them so they may recognize me. They are doing this because they do not recognize me." Still He prayed for the well-being of the dear ones.

When Prophet Mohammed was compelled to leave the city of Mecca, as he was leaving the city the people were standing with baskets full of dirt on both sides of the street where he was going to pass and they threw the rubbish on Prophet Mohammed. But instead of becoming upset at them, Prophet Mohammed said: "O Lord, forgive them."

And after Prophet Mohammed left that city, he went and sat in a cave in meditation. And the people who were opposing him followed him; they beat him and in a way killed him. From their side he was killed. But after that they thought, "Let us take out his teeth so he may not live after this." And at that time when they were trying to take out his teeth then also Prophet Mohammed uttered these words: "O Lord, forgive them."

Only he is a Gurumukh who doesn't become pleased or happy if God graciously gives him the kingdom of the three worlds. And if for some reason God takes back that kingdom, if he doesn't become displeased with God, only he is called a Gurumukh.

Those who keep enmity toward Him who is without enmity are never happy.

Now he says that Master is without enmity, He is gracious; and if someone becomes the enemy of such a person who has no enmity or jealousy towards anyone, then such a person becomes hollow from within.

Satguru wishes good for all. Why should bad things come to Him?
Nanak says, The Creator knows everything—nothing is hidden from Him.

Master always seeks the welfare of other people. And since He is in God's favor, even if people think ill of the Master, still no one can harm Him. God sees the Gurumukhs as well as the manmukhs. Nothing is hidden from God. Whatever karmas one has done, God makes us pay off those karmas.

No one can fool God. If after making mistakes, we throw that on some other person, and if we taunt other people, or blame other people, it doesn't mean that by doing that, God will accept what we are saying as coming from that person, and God will stop his progress. God sees everything, He has no enemies, and He always gives us what we are supposed to have. Masters have no enemies and God also has no enemies; and They always give us what we are supposed to have.

Mahatmas tell us that we look at other people's faults and laugh; but we never look at our own faults which have no beginning and no end.

He whom the Lord makes great is considered the Great One.
God forgives those with whom He is pleased, and they are liked by Him.

Only he becomes great who is made great by God. Only he is forgiven whom God Himself forgives. If God makes anyone great, if God makes anyone worth worshiping, only he is worshiped.

If anyone competes with Him he is an ignorant fool.

If anyone imitates one within whom God is manifested, saying, "Why do people worship Him and not me?" such a person is ignorant: he has no knowledge, and he is misled.

He whom the Master unites with Himself sings the Master's praise,
Nanak says, He who has understood and is absorbed in the True One is perfectly true.

Now, only he on whom God is gracious can meet the Master. No one has any control over the Master. No one can order the Master. We can get things from the Master only if He wants us to have them.

God is true, unaffected by Maya; the immortal One,
Without any fear, without any enmity, and formless.
Those who meditate on Him with one mind and one heart
Lose the burden of egoism.

Those who are selected by God and do the devotion of God, from their head the burden or veil of egoism is lifted and they have only God and Master within them.

Saints and Mahatmas are not equal to God, they are the dear children of God; and if the loving dear children want their Father to do anything, they can make their Father do anything they want.

Praise to the Gurumukhs and the Saints who have meditated on the Lord.
If one criticizes the Perfect Satguru, the whole world curses him.

Now He says, "I bow down to those who mold their lives according to the teachings of their Masters." And then Guru Ramdas Ji says that if anyone criticizes the Perfect Master who has molded His life according to the teachings of His Master, he doesn't get praised by the people and everyone curses him.

The Lord Himself resides in the Satguru and He Himself is the Protector.

Now He says, "Within the Satguru God is working, and God is manifested there. When God is manifested there, why should he worry about anything, why should he be afraid of anyone?" He says, "Oh Lord, if I lose my honor then also it is Your honor. If I am praised then You are praised."

Blessed are the ones who sing the praises of the Master. I salute them.
Nanak says, I sacrifice myself to those who meditate on the Creator.

Now He says, "Blessed is my Master, Guru Amardas, who did the meditation of Shabd Naam."

He Himself created the earth; He Himself created the sky,
He created the creatures and He Himself feeds them.

Often I have said that it is because of the Power of God working within us that our body is functioning. And when God withdraws His Power from our body, after that its features are useless: the eyes are still there, but they stop functioning. Only when the Power of God was working within our body were we able to use our hands to feed ourselves. That is why Guru Sahib says here that God has created all the creatures and He Himself is feeding them.

He Himself resides in everyone; He Himself is the abode of qualities.
Nanak says, Meditate on Naam so that all the sins may be cut.

God Himself resides in everyone and God Himself comes in the form of the Master. And He tells us that you can remove all the sins, if you meditate on the Shabd Naam.

Kabir Sahib says, "As soon as the Naam was kept in the heart, all the sins were burned off." It is just like lighting a match to a pile of dry grass.

Sehjo Bai also says, "Earlier, by making many mistakes, we collected a great burden of sins, but as soon as we came to the Master and surrendered to Him, in just a moment millions of our sins were removed."

You, the True Lord, are the Truth; the Truth is pleasing to You, the True One.
Those who praise You, the True One, the servants of Yama do not come near them.
Those within whose heart the True Lord is pleasing
Have bright faces in the court of the Lord.
The false ones are thrown back.
Those in whose hearts there is falsehood and deception,
They always get pain.
The faces of the false ones become black,
And the false ones become unreal.

Now He says, "O Lord, You are Truth, You are permanent, You never perish. Those who sing Your glory, those who come in contact with You, those who manifest You within, the Angels of Death never come to them." He says that there are those who have not done the devotion, not done the meditation, but still sit in front of people and say, "Come to us and we will liberate you." But God can never be deceived, and when such people will go to the Court of the Lord, He will not accept them; understanding them as waste or refuse, He will reject them and throw them out. Guru Nanak Sahib says that such people's condition is like that of the rat who cannot go through a hole by himself because the hole is too small. But with him he is carrying a big sifter and he wants to carry that sifter through the hole through which he himself cannot go. So this is the condition of those people who cannot themselves get liberation but promise liberation to others.

No one has been successful in deceiving God, and no one will ever be able to deceive God. The waste, or the refuse, get rejected there and God never accepts them.

Guru Nanak Sahib says that once the cranes imitated the swans. The swans fly in the air for a long time, but the cranes cannot. So looking at the swans, the cranes imitated them, and what was the result? The cranes were drowned in the ocean. The condition of those who don't do the devotion but still act as the Masters, their condition is like those cranes who try to imitate the swans but cannot fly. They imitate those who have become one with God, but because they have not become one with God, they always fail.

You can read the history of any Great Master of the past and you will find that all the Masters worked very hard; they did a lot of meditation. Guru Nanak Sahib meditated for eleven years in a very difficult situation; even though he was a Param Sant from the very beginning, still he meditated for eleven years and worked very hard.

Similarly, Guru Amardas used to serve His Master all day, and during the night He would stay up and do His meditation. That nail still exists to which Guru Amardas used to tie His hair when He would feel sleepy during the night in His meditation. He would tie His hair to the nail so He would not sleep. That nail still exists in India.

Hazur Swami Ji Maharaj, founder of the Radhasoami faith, meditated for seventeen years in a dark room. He used to lock Himself up in that room and meditate there.

In the same way Baba Jaimal Singh also worked very hard in His meditation. Whenever He would get hungry He would eat old food, making it wet by putting it in water; and after eating, again He would start doing His meditation.

There was one initiate of Baba Jaimal Singh whose name was also

Jaimal Singh. He was more than a hundred years old. And he used to come to me and tell me that Baba Jaimal Singh had a stick and whenever He would feel very sleepy He would beat Himself with that stick so that He would remain awake.

In the same way Baba Sawan Singh used to work very hard in His meditation and He also meditated a lot. He used to have one *bairagam*, a wooden stand, and He would stand and meditate whenever He would get bothered by sleep; and many times He would not come out of His room for two or three days continuously.

And there are still many other dear ones alive who know how Master Kirpal obeyed the commandments of His Master and worked very hard in His meditations. I have met many people who used to tell me, that if anyone wants to see the fruits of meditation they should go to Delhi and meet Kirpal Singh. They called Master Kirpal Singh a great meditator.

It was the same with Baba Bishan Das: Even though he had the knowledge of only two planes and had perfected only up to those two planes, still to achieve the perfection of two planes is also worthy. And the one who has perfected up to two planes, it is worth sacrificing for such a person. And I have seen Baba Bishan Das meditating: He had one wooden bench in which he had nails fixed, and whenever he would feel sleepy he would sit on those nails and meditate.

I myself have spent a large part of my life away from other people, underground; and I know what meditation is.

During the Second World War when Hitler was advancing everywhere, in India nobody was ready to join the army, because everybody was sent to fight with Hitler. And everyone was sure that those who would go to fight with Hitler would never come back and death was certain for them. But I was very happy in giving my name to go there. At that time I was very young and those who were seeing me were very surprised, looking at my courage. They would say, "Look at that young boy. He is so young but still he wants to go and fight and he is ready to sacrifice himself." Before going to the front, when we were sent for the medical check-up, the doctor asked our commander who should be recommended for having milk. The commander felt very sorry for all of us and said, "They are all the goats of sacrifice, so it is better if they can have milk in their last days."

So that was such a time when nobody wanted to go the front. I was feeling very good about going to the front, and I was very willing to do that because I was very courageous. And I was feeling proud of that also: that I was going to the front when nobody else wanted to do that. At that time people would accept imprisonment for twenty years, but would not go and join the army. But I saw it as a very easy thing to do. But later on when I went underground for meditation, I know how difficult it was for me to meditate, and how much easier it was for me to go to the front and sacrifice my life. Because when we meditate, the mind comes and stands in front of us like a tiger and tells us, "Now I will not let you go within." Mind is such a strong enemy that you have to fight with him daily. Meditation is just like inviting your mind to fight with you. Those who have stayed up in the night and have suffered a lot of pain, those who have given much pain to their body for meditation, they know meditation is a very difficult thing to do.

Tulsi Sahib says, "To fight in the battlefield may be the work of a day or two, but to fight with the mind is a battle which you have to do always with no sword or weapon."

Kabir Sahib said, "By enjoying and laughing nobody has ever achieved the Beloved God. If Beloved God could be achieved easily, then what would be the use of suffering all these pains?"

So we should be courageous, we should work hard, and we should never become lazy in our hard work.

The Satguru has the quality of the earth: As one sows in it, such a fruit he gets.
The disciples of the Master sow the seeds of nectar and get the fruit of the nectar from the Lord.
Their faces are bright in this world and beyond, and they get the true honor in the court of the Lord.
In the heart of some is falsehood, and they continuously practice falsehood.
As they sow such seeds, such a fruit they will get.
When the Satguru, the Jeweler, looks closely at them, they will be revealed as counterfeit.
They get always what they bring about; they sound as God makes them sound.
Nanak says, In both sides the Lord Himself works, and daily He sees everything.
Mind is one, and it can work in one direction. Wherever he is attached, he gets that place.
Someone may talk about many things, but he only gets what he has at home.
Without the Satguru one doesn't get the right understanding.
Egoism does not flee from within.
The egotists have suffering and hunger
And they beg from door to door.
Falsehood and deceit do not remain hidden.
The outward show and covering fall off.

For whom it is pre-written, him the Satguru,
the Lord, meets.
As when iron is brought in contact with the
Philosopher's Stone,
Through that meeting it becomes gold.
O Lord of humble Nanak, you are the Lord.
As it pleases you, you make things seen.
The Lord Himself unites them with Him
who serve Him in their hearts.
They share the good qualities, and with the
Shabd they burn their bad qualities.
The bad qualities are thrown away, and to
whom God gives the true qualities,
(they) get those.
I sacrifice myself to my Master, Who has
manifested the good qualities, removing
the bad ones.
Great is the Glory of the Great One:
Gurumuks sing His praise.

3

The Sight of the Perfect Master

The Satguru has the quality of the earth: As one sows in it, such a fruit he gets.
The disciples of the Master sow the seeds of nectar and get the fruit of the nectar from the Lord.

God is not the personal property of anyone; He belongs to every community, He belongs to every religion, He belongs to every country. And everybody in this world—whether he is man or woman, whether he belongs to this country or that country, or whether he comes from lower class or upper class—all have the right to realize Him. Masters are sent by God and that is why they also belong to every religion. Masters make us understand that Satgurus are like the earth: If you sow sugar cane in the earth or if you sow chilies or if you sow wheat —whatever you sow, you will reap only that. In the same way, whatever feelings you have for the Master, you get the fruit according to your feelings.

Masters tell us, whatever karma you do you will have to suffer or enjoy the reaction of that. Whatever you sow, that will be grown and you will have to reap that. We cannot harvest sugar cane after planting chilies. Nor can we harvest chilies by sowing sugar cane. Kabir Sahib says, "If the farmer sows a useless bush and expects to harvest sugar cane, he cannot do that; because whatever you sow, that you will reap."

But Satguru is the soil or ground of religion, and whatever you sow in Him, you get that. Gurumukhs always sow the nectar of Naam in Him, and that is why they get to drink that nectar of Naam. Farid Sahib says, "Sugar, rock candy, honey and other things are very sweet, but Naam—the Name of the Lord—is sweeter than this, and no other sweet thing can compare with it."

Their faces are bright in this world and beyond, and they get the true honor in the court of the Lord.

Guru Ramdas Ji says, "Those who do the meditation of Shabd Naam and make their soul free from the clutches of mind, they live very happily and comfortably in this world. And when they leave this world and go to the court of the Lord, there also they are very welcome and God honors them."

> **In the heart of some is falsehood, and they continuously practice falsehood.**
> **As they sow such seeds, such a fruit they will get.**
> **When the Satguru, the Jeweler, looks closely at them, they will be revealed as counterfeit.**

In the Sangat of the Satgurus, dear souls, loving souls, come, and in addition many other souls also come just from looking at other people. In the *Mansarovar,* or the pure pool, the swans go as well as the cranes. Swans go there to search for pearls, but the cranes go there searching for fish. But when they do not get the fish, they leave disappointed. So such souls, those who are the slaves of their mind and the organs of senses, even if they come to the Satsang of the Master, even if they spend a lot of time there, still within them they have the quality of the crane and do not accept the words of the Master as the loving souls do.

The sight of the Saints is the sight of the Perfect Jeweler; They can very well see who is supposed to be in the Sangat and who is not supposed to be there. So when those souls who are not supposed to be in their Sangat come to their Satsang, they do one or another thing, looking at which only the dear souls remain in the Satsang, while the other people don't have love for the Master after that, and they leave the Satsang. Hazrat Bahu says, "Bitter squash will never turn into watermelon, no matter if you take it to Mecca, the holy place." In the same way, even if you go on putting millions of tons of sugar in a salt well, still the water will not turn sweet.

In Agra, in the Satsang of Swami Ji Maharaj, many "flies"—people who were not supposed to be there—started coming. They would come to eat the food and do other things, but they would have no faith in the Master. So in order to remove those flies, once Swami Ji Maharaj took some water in His mouth and spit that water on the food which had just been made in the langar. For the dear ones it was a blessing, and they thought, "This is the most fortunate day when the Master has 'contaminated' all the food and He has made this parshad." But those people who had no faith in the Master were upset; they said, "What is the use of coming to this place where we are fed contaminated food?"

And they left. Some people used to say when Master Sawan Singh was alive, "No use to go there because he will give you dirty food to eat." And some people say now, that we do not bless the food but contaminate it.* So Masters do such things to keep the flies out of their Satsang.

Once Master Sawan Singh was giving Satsang in Shimla, and there came some Akalis. (Akalis are a politically and religiously militant sect of the Sikh religion.) They used to come there and oppose Master Sawan Singh very much. When they came, the Satsang was going on. So Master Sawan Singh welcomed them and told them that if they wanted to talk to him, he could stop giving Satsang and see them. But they said, "No, you keep doing the Satsang, and after the Satsang is over we will see you." After the Satsang was over and when the time came to distribute the parshad, those people did not accept the parshad, and they asked, "First you should tell us whether this parshad, this food, is contaminated or whether it is fresh." So Master Sawan Singh replied, "It is both. It is fresh as well as contaminated." They said, "How is that possible?" Master Sawan Singh replied, "You see, when you offer the parshad, after doing your worship—when you offer some food to God and say, 'Oh God, please take some from this and turn the rest into parshad'—if God accepts that, it means that it is contaminated because God has eaten from the same plate. And if God does not accept that, it means that it is fresh. So in whatever way you want, you can understand this." Then they realized that when a Master touches the food He is not contaminating it, He is blessing it and they were convinced that Masters do not contaminate any food. Master Sawan Singh said, "You can ask my sons: I never made them eat with me from the same plate." A Master who has stayed up all night and has meditated a lot, and who has earned the wealth of spirituality by working very hard, how would he like to give this wealth of spirituality to other people: By allowing them to eat from his plate, or by allowing them to eat contaminated food?

In the same way, when Guru Nanak wanted to remove the flies, He disguised Himself as a hunter, and he took some dogs with him and he had a sword in his hand. He told his disciples to follow him; but when his disciples saw him as a hunter, they felt very bad, and one by one they all left him. Everyone went away from him except Bhai

* According to Hindu religious law, to touch food in any way by anyone of a lower caste than the person eating it is defiling it. The custom of giving parshad by the Masters, many of whom were of very low caste, grew up in the teeth of this law.

Lena, who was later on called Guru Angad. When Guru Nanak asked him why he was following him and did not go away like the others, he replied, "The other people went because they might have something to do in the world, but I have nothing in the world which I can say is my own, except You; You are the only thing which belongs to me. That is why I am with You." Guru Nanak was so pleased with him that he showered all his Grace on Guru Angad.

The Perfect Masters, those who have done the meditation, don't desire many disciples. They are not in this world to collect many disciples. They look only for the loving souls. Master Sawan Singh used to say, "It is much better to have one faithful disciple than to have one thousand disciples who don't have faith in the Master."

As we get the Perfect Master only if we are very fortunate ones; in the same way, Master only gets a good disciple if He is very fortunate. If Perfect Masters didn't get perfect disciples, then nobody could recognize Their glory in this world, because you know that the worldly people cannot recognize the Masters. Only the perfect disciples can recognize the Masters. So that is why Guru Ramdas Ji Maharaj says here, "Master has the sight of a jeweler, and when He looks at the people he knows who is good for Him and who is not; who is supposed to come in His sangat and who is not." That is why, when he wants to remove those people from his sangat who are not supposed to be there, he does such things. And in that way, he removes the flies.

They get always what they bring about; they sound as God makes them sound.
Nanak says, "In both sides the Lord Himself works, and daily He sees everything."

Within the Gurumukhs God resides, and manmukhs also are created by God. God is the protector of both of them; God takes care of both of them. But because Gurumukhs do the devotion of God in order to reach God, they get the wealth of devotion of God and do reach Him. Whereas the manmukhs are driven by passions and desire worldly things; therefore they get to enjoy those, which lead them to hell. So whatever feeling you have when you are doing the devotion to the Lord, you get the fruit according to that.

This world is like a big shopping center, in which everybody is either selling his goods, or buying goods from the world. Everybody is doing his work, whatever work he has been given, good or bad. Suppose one wise man went to a shopping center with his son, and was called bad names by someone who was selling things in the market. His son doesn't know what he is doing, so he complains to his father: "Father, look at that man. He is saying bad things to you. Why don't you reply to him?" But the father is wise; he knows that those bad names are not good for him, and he is not a customer of them. So he says, "Never mind, my son; let's go. Everybody in this market is selling his things, but we don't want to take this, so why worry about it? There is no need to pay any attention to it." Because that father was wise, he explained to his son also, and he was not affected by the bad things which were said to him in the market of this world.

In the same way, when Masters come They know what is good for Them and what is bad for Them. And even if people criticize Them and say bad words to Them, They don't respond in the same tone; They pay no attention to that. Because They know that neither criticism of this world is going to go with Them, nor the praise or honor of this world. The only thing which will accompany us is the Naam of the Master and the devotion of the Naam which we have done in this world. Masters also come in this world, this shopping center, and They also do many things; but They never accept those things which are harmful to Them; They never pay any attention to any criticism or any bad things which people offer to them.

Mind is one, and it can work in one side. Wherever he is attached, he gets that place.
Someone may talk about many things, but he only gets what he has at home.

You have only one mind, and you can make him do anything you want. If you want, you can make him do the devotion of the Lord, and if you want, you can make him enjoy the worldly pleasures. It is not possible for you to criticize others and backbite others, and at the same time realize God. You can do only one thing; either you involve your mind in criticism, in doing bad things and enjoying worldly things; or you can involve him in, or make him do, the devotion of the Lord. Guru Sahib says, "When the taste of the devotion of the Lord comes, then the taste of the worldly pleasures finds no place there." Mahatmas make us understand that God cannot be realized by talking about Him, or by hearing stories, or telling stories about Him. Whatever receptivity you have within you, according to that you can realize God.

Master Sawan Singh used to say, "You go within and see the condition of authors of books which are very popular in this world – go and see how the Negative Power has tortured them. Because writing books and giving talks is the work of the mind and the intellect." Just because we have read many books, or written many books, it doesn't mean that God will open His door to us, because all these works are of mind and intellect. We can make God open his doors to us only by doing the practices which are shown to us by our Master.

Master Kirpal often used to tell the story of the pundit, or learned scholar, who came to Kabir Sahib carrying a lot of books on a bullock, to debate with him. In those days they had no other means of transportation: jeeps, cars, etc. So they had to carry their things on the backs of bullocks, or other animals. So he came with all the books he had on the bullock. And when he came to the house of Kabir Sahib, Kabir was not there but his daughter, Kamali, was there. So he asked her, "Is this the house of Kabir Sahib?" She replied, "Kabir's home is in the sky, and the path which goes to Kabir's home is very slippery. Not even an ant can go there. O Pundit, what makes you think you can get there with so many books and a bullock?"

Nowadays in India, there are many universities. But in the olden days there was only one university, in the city of Kashi. Those who graduated from that university were greatly honored because they were supposed to be very great learned people. Once it so happened that two scholars, after graduating from that university, were on the way back to their home, and had to spend the night in one farmer's home. When they arrived there, the farmer welcomed them very warmly and allowed them to spend the night there. Maybe to attend the call of nature, one of those scholars went out. So the farmer asked the other scholar how learned the scholar was who had just gone out. (You know that one scholar will never praise another; he says, "He doesn't know anything, only I know.") So that scholar replied; "Well, he doesn't know anything. He is a donkey. I am more learned than he is." After some time, the one who had gone out came back; and the one who was in the house went out. So the farmer asked that same question to that scholar. And he said, "Well, I am the most learned man. He is a bull, he is not a scholar." So the farmer kept quiet. And when the food was ready and he invited them to eat, instead of serving them food for humans, in one plate he had put some grass and leaves, and in the other plate he had hay. They got very upset and said, "O farmer, why don't you bring the food which we want to eat?" The farmer replied, "You said that he is a donkey, so I have brought donkey food for him; and you said that he is a bull, and I have brought the bull's food for him." When they realized they had criticized each other and had praised only themselves, they felt very embarrassed, and they left without eating. Master Kirpal Singh Ji used to tell this story very often just to make the learned people understand that by learning, by becoming scholars, you cannot develop humility; by getting a lot of knowledge and becoming scholars, you just wrestle with your mind and it doesn't add to your humility.

Kabir Sahib even says, "O learned one, you have come to meet me and you are quoting from many books, but how long are you going to survive by eating other people's leftover foods?" He explains: "People come to the Master and quote from one book or another; they quote from the books in which the experiences of the perfect Masters are written. But how long are we going to survive if we don't practice those words in *our* life, and if we don't mold our life according to that?" Only reading of the experiences of the Masters will not do any good to us. Unless we practice them, we will not be able to progress.

Master Sawan Singh Ji used to say that once a Master was walking, and another man was also with him. Both of them saw that many animals were coming: cows and buffaloes and sheep were coming, and a shepherd was leading them. So the man who was with that Master became very happy, and said, "Master, look at that! How many animals are coming!" Master was very patient and said, "Well, there are many coming, but what have you to do with that? Do you have any animal of your own in there?" He said, "No, I have no animal there, but my uncle's cow is there." He replied, "Then why are you worried about it? Why are you so happy? You don't have anything in there."

So Masters tell us, we should first be concerned for our own soul. We should know how far we go in meditation and how far we can withdraw our soul. First we should worry about our own selves. Just by reading other people's experiences we should not get excited. Reading is not bad, but you should understand the *meaning* of reading also. You should read that, and you should put that into practice: you should work for your own soul.

Guru Sahib calls that learned one foolish who has greed and egoism. Mahatmas do not mean to say that reading is not good, or learning is not good, or getting knowledge is not good. They say that it is good to get knowledge, it is good to read (You see that now we are also reading this bani). But they say that whatever you read you should understand, and you should put that into practice. Only that reading is worthwhile which you put into practice after reading.

Without the Satguru one doesn't get the right understanding.
Egoism does not flee from within.
The egotists have suffering and hunger
And they beg from door to door.

Without the guidance of the Master we cannot know about our Real Home; and without the guidance of the Master, we cannot know what is good for us and what is bad for us. Without the guidance of the Master we cannot get rid of the disease of egoism. Those who are bothered by the ego always have pain, take birth, die, and always come and go in this world.

Namdev was a calico printer, born in a low caste. In India in those days people believed very strongly in the caste system, and they did not allow people of low caste to enter the temple of the high-caste people. But Namdev was very interested in doing the devotion of the Lord. Once in a state of intoxication, he went into a temple and sat there. When the other people came and saw that one low-caste man was sitting there in the devotion of the Lord, in the temple, they became very upset and they threw Namdev out of that temple and made Him sit behind it. Because Namdev was doing meditation and sitting in the remembrance of God, as soon as he connected himself with God the front door of that temple was turned in the direction in which Namdev was sitting. The people were very surprised; they had been singing and chanting hymns and playing musical instruments to please God. But God was not pleased by their devotion; He was pleased by Namdev's devotion – so pleased that He turned the door of the temple in His direction. When Namdev saw that the other people were singing, and playing cymbals and other things, he had no musical instrument to play with, but he also felt like playing some music; so he took off his sandals and started playing music with them. God is realized only in a state of innocence. When we are innocent, only then God showers Grace on us.

This incident of Namdev happened in the village called Ghuman which means "turned around," and it was the same village where Baba Jaimal Singh was born. So Guru Nanak Sahib says, "God turns his back on the critics and egoistic people; but those who meditate on Naam, He embraces them."

> **Falsehood and deceit do not remain hidden.**
> **The outward show and covering fall off.**
> **For whom it is pre-written, him the Satguru, the Lord, meets.**

We cannot hide untrue or false things for long. The ornament which has a gold plating but in fact is not made of gold, can pretend that it is made of gold until it is taken to the jeweler. But as soon as the jeweler sees it and tests it, he will know that it is not gold, but something else.

No one can deceive God and Master, because both of Them are sitting within us. They know how much love we have for Them, and how much we are pretending to be Their lovers.They know how true we are. That is why we can never deceive them. That is why in the Satsang They say, "Be holy and be pure." Because the more holy you are and the purer you are, the closer you will come to God. The only way of making yourself holy and of purifying yourself is Simran. Simran purifies our soul, and contemplation or dhyan makes it possible for our soul to remain fixed at the eye center; and after that the Shabd pulls our soul up. So Masters always say, "Keep your mind involved in doing Simran so that your soul may get more purified and be able to rise above."

He says, "Satguru meets only them in whose fate it is written from the beginning."

As when iron is brought in contact with the Philosopher's Stone,
Through that meeting it becomes gold.

Now Guru Ramdas Ji very lovingly explains to us that if we touch iron with a philosopher's stone, it is turned into gold. In the same way, no matter how bad we are, how many bad deeds we have done, if we come in the Satsang of the Master, if we obey His commandments, and if we do what He is telling us to do and everything that we are supposed to do, no matter how bad we are, after coming in the Sangat of Master we can become good.

But Kabir Sahib says, "Oh Kabir, what can the philosopher's stone do if the iron is rusty?" What can the Master do if the disciple is still obeying the dictates of the mind and is involved in the pleasures of the organs of senses? What is the fault in the philosopher's stone if the iron is rusted?

Oh Lord of humble Nanak, you are the Lord.
As it pleases you, you make things seen.

"Oh Lord, You are the Giver to everyone and you are the Protector of everyone; and it is all in Your will. Whatever way You want You are taking care of the souls." Some get the awareness of what they have to do, and some do not get that awareness and are still wandering here and there. Some people come to the Master and realize that now they are to do the meditation and go back Home. Whereas some people come to the Master, but still don't realize that it is their duty to do the meditation and go back Home.

The Lord Himself unites them with Him who serve Him in their hearts.
They share the good qualities, and with the Shabd they burn their bad qualities.

Now Guru Ramdas Ji describes the glory of the Lord. He says, "Oh Lord, those who do your devotion, You give them a place in Your Home. And those who manifest You within, and go to them who have manifested You within, they also share the good qualities, and they also share the knowledge about You, by going in their company."

The bad qualities are thrown away, and to whom God gives the true qualities, (they) get those.

When we thresh the crop, we pay no attention to its cover or husk; we are just concerned about collecting the grain. Or when we eat almonds, we take out the almonds and throw away the shell; we just take the fruit and eat that. In the same way, when we do the devotion of Shabd Naam, we put all our attention on the inner fruit, and pay no attention to the worldly pleasures and things. Because all these worldly pleasures seem useless when we get interested in doing the meditation of Naam.

I sacrifice myself to my Master, Who has manifested the good qualities, removing the bad ones.

He says, "I sacrifice myself for my brave Master, Who made me develop the good habits within myself and leave the bad habits. It is only because of His grace and mercy that now I can see what things are useless and what are useful." For spiritual progress it is very important to have a pure mind.

Great is the Glory of the Great One:
Gurumukhs sing His praise.

When we rise above the rajagun, tamagun and satagun, and remove all the vestures—physical, astral and causal covers —from our soul, then we are able to meet God. And the Gurumukhs Who reach Sach Khand and become one with God never say even a single word in Their own praise. When They utter anything, it is all in the praise of Their Master, it is all in the praise of God. And that is why They say, "I have no mission, I have no work to do; whatever I have in this world, that all belongs to God. And in whatever way God wants me to work, I am working in that way."

Guru Nanak Sahib says, "All the glory is to the Greater One. All the glory is to my Master, Who taught me the Path of the Naam and told me what was my work in this. So whatever I have done, whatever I have achieved, I sing His praise; all the glory, all the credit, goes to Him."

Kabir Sahib says, "It is like a piece of salt, who went into the ocean to see where it came from—to find its origin. And when it went there, it was dissolved there, and now it doesn't come back to tell people what its origin was."

The Great Glory is in that Satguru who meditates
daily on the Naam of the Lord.
By meditating on the Naam of the Lord,
purity is achieved;
And one gets satiated by the Naam of the Lord.
The Naam of the Lord is strength, the Naam
of the Lord is the Support;
And the only Protector is the Naam of the Lord.
Those who worship the form of the Master
attentively get as fruits their heart's desire.
Those who criticize the perfect Satguru, the
Creator will cause them to be killed;
Then that time does not come in his hands
again.
Whatever he sows, he himself reaps.
He is carried to the severe hell with a black
face and garroted like the thieves.
If he takes refuge in Satguru again, then he is
saved
If he meditates on the Naam of the Lord.
Nanak speaks the words of the Lord, the
Creator, as may please the Lord.
He who does not obey the order of a Perfect
Master is manmukh, ignorant, false,
and is robbed by maya, the poison.
Within him is falsehood, and false under-
standing;
He is involved in useless disputes.

He sells many talks, but no one is pleased with his talking.
He goes from home to home like an unfaithful wife.
Those who come in contact with him get stained.
Gurumukhs work differently from them. They give up the critic's company, and sit near the Master.
He who hides his Master is not a good man.
O Saints, he has lost the capital and profit.
Nanak talked about Vedas and Shastras (and said),
The Word of the Perfect Master is above all.
The disciples of the Master like the Glory of the Perfect Master.
Manmukhs do not have that opportunity in their hands.
The Perfect True One is greater than all.
He whom the Satguru appoints, obtains Him.
He who meditates on the truth is the Satguru, and the True One and the Satguru are one.
He who has controlled the five dacoits is the Satguru.
Those who make themselves count without serving the Satguru, their faces are dull-curse on their faces.
No one is pleased by what they speak.

Their faces are black because of deviating from the Satguru.
The whole field belongs to the Lord, and He Himself does the farming.
Blessing the Gurumukhs, He germinates (their field) whereas the manmukhs lose the seed.
Everyone sows for his own advantage, but that field which is pleasing to the Lord is made to germinate.
The disciples of the Master always sow the seeds of the Lord, and get the nectarful fruit of Naam.
Yama, the mouse, is constantly gnawing at the field.
The Creator, the Lord, chases him away.
The field was made to germinate by the Love of the Lord;
And with the Grace of the Lord, piles of corn were grown.
Those who meditate on the Satguru, their anxiety and worry are removed.
Nanak says, He who meditates on Naam swims across and makes the whole world swim across.
The whole day the manmukh is involved in greed and other things.
In the night he is buried in sleep. All the nine organs of senses make him weak.

The manmukhs always obey the orders of their
spouses, and daily they bring good things to them.
Those who do what they are told by their spouses
are impure, foolish, and without any
intellect.
Those who do things after asking their spouses—
Within them lust is spread.
He who walks when the Satguru tells him is
the true person—
Better than the best one.
The women and men are all created by Him.
This is all the play of the Lord.
Nanak says, Everything is Your creation—You
are better than the best one.
You are unconcerned, deep, inestimable—how
can we appraise you?
Those who have met the Satguru and meditate
on You are the fortunate ones.
The Bani of the Satguru is the form of truth.
One becomes the Bani of the Master.
Those who imitate the Satguru and speak the
imperfect Bani are the false ones,
And with their falsehood they fall down.
In their heart they have one thing—in their
head they have something else.
They die in grief, being involved in Maya,
the poison.

4

The Harvest of Nectar

The Great Glory is in that Satguru who meditates daily on the Naam of the Lord.

On the first day I said that this is the bani of Guru Ramdas Ji Maharaj, and that I will do Satsang on this very bani for ten or twelve days—as long as I am here, (at Sant Bani Ashram) I will continue doing satsang on this bani. In this bani, the love which Guru Ramdas had for His Master, Guru Amardas, is described. And moreover, whatever Guru Amardas had to go through and whatever He had to suffer because the people were opposing Him, whatever He had to face, how much He was criticized, etc., is also described. Lovers always talk about their beloved; that is why here Guru Ramdas Ji is talking about His Master, His Beloved.

Now Guru Ramdas asks, "What is the greatness of the Master? Why is He loved and liked by everyone?" He says that the greatness of Master is that He is always in connection with God, whether He is sitting or standing, whether He is asleep or awake; He always remains in tune with God. This is the greatness of the Master: that God Himself is manifested within Him.

By meditating on the Naam of the Lord, purity is achieved;
And one gets satiated by the Naam of the Lord.

The desire of the Master is Naam. The thing which contents Him also is Naam. He is always absorbed in Naam. By meditating on Naam and by achieving Naam, He always remains contented in Naam.

The Naam of the Lord is the strength, the Naam of the Lord is the Support;
And the only Protector is the Naam of the Lord.

Naam is His protector, Naam is His support, Naam is His honor. Whatever He has, that all is of Naam.

> **Those who worship the form of the Master attentively get as fruits their heart's desire.**

Those who go in the company of such Masters, those who meditate on such Masters, those who do the devotion of such Masters Whose food is Naam and Who get contented by doing the meditation of Naam and within whom Naam is manifested; such people—those who are desirous of Naam—get all their desires fulfilled as well as getting Naam. Whatever fruits we ask for, we get that from our Satguru.

> **Those who criticize the perfect Satguru, the Creator will cause them to be killed;**
> **Then that time does not come in his hands again.**
> **Whatever he sows, he himself reaps.**

Now Guru Ramdas Ji Maharaj says that God doesn't give any place at His feet to a person who criticizes such a Master; He makes them get a beating from the angels of death. While he is getting the beating, then he repents. But once the time is lost, he cannot gain it back. He repents, but it is no use.

> **He is carried to the severe hell with a black face and garroted like the thieves.**

He says, that not only does such a person get a beating from the angels of death; besides that, he is handcuffed and tied and thrown into hell, just like thieves when they are caught red-handed are thrown into prison.

> **If he takes refuge in Satguru again, then he is saved**
> **If he meditates on the Naam of the Lord.**

We got the human body in order to do devotion of the Lord; but instead of doing that, we started criticizing other people, and we made a lot of bad karmas, as a result of which we go to hell. But if that critic, after suffering in hell, comes back in the world and gets a body, if he comes to the feet of the Master, and does the meditation of Naam, only then can he get liberation. If he doesn't do that, he will keep coming in bodies and he will keep having the pain of birth and death.

Nanak speaks the words of the Lord, the Creator, as may please the Lord.

Now Guru Ramdas Ji says that He is not saying all of these things to frighten people. "Because I go to God and I see what is happening in the Court of God, in order to make people understand, I am saying all of these things. I am not saying them to frighten anyone."

He who does not obey the order of a Perfect Master is Manmukh, ignorant, false, and is robbed by Maya, the poison.

Now Guru Ramdas Ji says that all of the Saints and Masters Who came on this physical plane told us to abstain from criticism. They all told us to stop committing sins, and They all told us to leave backbiting and bad deeds. So He says that if you love the Master, and obey the commandments of the Master, then we should definitely refrain from such bad habits. Criticism is not good. It only pleases your mind. Those who criticize others, their faces will be blackened and they will be sent to hell.

Hazur Maharaj Kirpal Singh Ji used to say, "If you love me, keep my commandments." So Guru Ramdas Ji says that the one who doesn't obey the commandments of the perfect Master is ignorant, he is foolish, he is *manmukh*, and he is following his mind.

Within him is falsehood, and false understanding;
He is involved in useless disputes.

He who does not love the perfect Masters and does not obey Their commandments, he is *manmukh*, and he is always involved in telling lies. He speaks lies, he hears lies, and all day long his dealing is with untruth. Master Sawan Singh Ji used to say that criticism is neither sour nor sweet, but it cuts the root of our spirituality. He even used to say that whoever you criticize, all his sins will come into your account, and all your good deeds will be transferred into his account.

He sells many talks, but no one is pleased with his talking.

The manmukh, who doesn't obey the commandments of the Master, talks a lot. But the pity is that nobody relies on his talking, because he is a manmukh. Once Master Sawan Singh Ji went to a town to hold Satsang. The organizers asked Him if they could put up some posters or make some announcements, so that people would know. Master Sawan Singh Ji replied, "You don't have to do that, because those who are supposed to do this work of letting people know that I am here, will do that even without your asking." And it happened, because the Arya Samajis and Akalis, those who used to oppose Master Sawan Singh Ji a lot, started criticizing Him. They had loud speakers fitted on the jeeps, and they went all around the city, saying, "Don't go to see the Master of Radhasoami because He is a magician and will put a musical instrument in your head. He will win you over by His magic, so don't go there." So people, out of curiosity, went to see Master Sawan Singh, and once they came to see Him, they became His. Master Sawan Singh, when He heard that people were doing this negative publicity, called the organizers and asked them, "Do you see how they are doing the work for you?" Master Kirpal Singh used to say that at that very satsang, the canopy which was set up was so full, it was jampacked, and many people had to stand outside. Many more came than they were expecting. They all went away very happy and thanked the Arya Samajis and the Akalis for telling them about this perfect Master.

He goes from home to home like an unfaithful wife.
Those who come in contact with him get stained.

Now Guru Ramdas Ji says that the critic of the Master doesn't stay at one place. He goes from home to home, and he goes on criticizing the Master. His condition is that of the unfaithful wife who is not loyal to her husband, and goes from one man to another. You know that the friends of such a woman also get stained. In the same way, those who spend time in the company of such a critic of the Master also get blamed.

Gurumukhs work differently from them. They give up the critic's company, and sit near the Master.

Now He says that the loving souls don't even like to touch the shadow of such critics. Giving up the company and friendship of such people, they always remain in the refuge of the Master. Tulsi Sahib says, "If God becomes the critic of the Master, don't even go to see Him."

He who hides his Master is not a good man.
O Saints, he has lost the capital and profit.

Those who hide their Master are not good.

Nanak talked about Vedas and Shastras (and said),

The Word of the Perfect Master is above all.

You can read the writings of Guru Nanak, and there also you will find that He has quoted from many Vedas and Shastras, holy scriptures. And quoting from them He has told us that the Master is above all, and the Word of the Master should be obeyed. The Word of the Master should be accepted as the greatest thing of all.

The disciples of the Master like the Glory of the Perfect Master.
Manmukhs do not have that opportunity in their hands.

The perfect disciples of the Master always like to sing the glory of the Master. They are very pleased when they see that many people come and get benefit from the presence of their Master. Whereas the manmukhs do not like this. They don't like that their Master should be praised and glorified in the world. That is why they always try to hide Him. Master Kirpal Singh, the true Lord Himself, told me this: "I had no interest in this world. I had no interest in coming out. But I am just obeying the word of the Master. Master Sawan Singh told me, 'Don't let my teachings remain hidden in this world.' "

The Perfect True One is greater than all.
He whom the Satguru appoints, obtains Him.

God is greater than all. God is above all. God is the Giver. God is everywhere, but who can manifest such a God within him? Only those who have the Grace of Master and only those who are chosen by Him. When Master decides that someone should have the complete knowledge of God and that God should be manifested in Him—only such a person can manifest God within him. Otherwise nobody can do it.

He who meditates on the truth is the Satguru, and the True One and the Satguru are one.

Earlier Guru Ramdas said that this is the greatness of the Master, that within Him Naam is manifested. Now He says that by doing the meditation of Naam, Master and God become one.

He who has controlled the five dacoits is the Satguru.
Those who make themselves count without serving the Satguru, their faces are dull—curse on their faces.

He is the Satguru or the true Master Who has controlled lust, anger, greed, attachment, and egoism by meditating on Shabd Naam. He who has not done any meditation, but still tells people, "I am the Master,"—always understand that he is lying. Such a person is tasteless from within and from outside also.

No one is pleased by what they speak.
Their faces are black because of deviating from the Satguru.

The loving souls always remain away from such people who pretend to be more than they are, because they are thrown out by the Master because they didn't obey His commandments. What are the commandments of the Master? Master told us to do the meditation of Naam, to rise above lust, anger, and these passions. Those who don't do that, who don't obey His commandments, are not appreciated anywhere. The dear souls who love the Master always remain away from such people. Kabir Sahib said about those who teach others without teaching themselves first, that sand will come into their mouths. And if they are taking care of other people's fields while their own courtyard is on fire, they are foolish.

The whole field belongs to the Lord, and He Himself does the farming.
Blessing the Gurumukhs, He germinates (their field) whereas the manmukhs lose the seed.

This world is like a farm of God. The gurumukhs sow and collect the wealth of Naam. Whereas the manmukhs misuse and lose whatever capital they have been given. When they go back to God, they are empty-handed.

Everyone sows for his own advantage, but that field which is pleasing to the Lord is made to germinate.
The disciples of the Master always sow the seeds of the Lord, and get the nectarful fruit of Naam.

In this world everybody is farming, and those who are obeying their minds are involving themselves in worldly pleasures and reap the fruit of that. Whereas those who are doing the farming of Naam, (because the daily meditation which we do is like farming) get a harvest of what? We get the nectar. Nectar is that by drinking which we become immortal. Those who are sent or who do the devotion of the Lord, harvest the nectar, drink, and become immortal, and they become free from the pain of birth and death.

You know that when we want to sow anything, first of all, we prepare the ground; and after cultivating it, only then we sow the seed. Later on it sprouts, and then we take good care of it. After a lot of time, during which we keep taking care of it, we harvest it. In the same way, the daily meditation, Simran, or whatever we are doing to prepare ourselves, is like preparing the ground; and when the ground is prepared, then the seed of Naam which is within us, sprouts, and we harvest that Nectar.

Don't think that whatever meditation you are doing, whether it is little or more, is going useless. Even if you don't get any experience, still the meditation, or the time which you are spending in the meditation, is all counted in the devotion. If after working so hard and meditating a lot, still the door is not opened to us, it means that we are not yet ready to enter the kingdom of the Lord. But even then we should not leave the door of the Lord; because if we keep sitting there, definitely one day God will open His door to us. And whatever Simran you do—even if you do Simran once—that also is counted. God preserves our devotion, He preserves our meditation, and He will definitely give us the fruit of it one day.

Yama, the mouse, is constantly gnawing at the field.
The Creator, the Lord, chases him away.
The field was made to germinate by the Love of the Lord;
And with the Grace of the Lord, piles of corn were grown.

When we sow the seeds, after that we need to make a fence around our field to protect our crop from other people. Later on if insects come and bother and start eating our crop, we use something to protect our crop from them. And those who have done farming know that sometimes mice get into the field, and they can destroy the crop. The farmer is not careless—after sowing the seeds he always takes care of the field—so he comes there and protects the crop from those mice also. In that way he takes care of the crop, and eventually he harvests it.

In the same way, when Master does the farming of Naam, He is also not careless after sowing the seed. After the seed of Naam which is sown within us sprouts, as we are growing in our devotion, then these mice and insects also come. What is the mouse which comes within us and destroys our meditation? That is the Negative Power; he is residing within us and he always tries to destroy the crop, the Naam, which we have within us. But this crop cannot be destroyed because Master is always watching us. He doesn't become careless. He is also sitting within us; and when he sees that the mouse is giving us a very hard time and we are helpless in front of him and have no way out, then Master Himself helps us. He has to harvest this crop of Naam within us, so He doesn't become careless. He protects us from this Negative Power, He helps us, and He always takes care of us.

Now if every single grain of any crop is collected, it makes a big pile. In the same way, the Simran and meditation which we are doing, every single repetition of Naam, is counted, and Master preserves it like the farmer preserves the seeds of grain. When we are able to protect that by ourselves, then Master gives us the wealth of our devotion, of our meditation. When we see that all the meditation and all the Simran which we were doing was preserved and that every single repetition was counted and was preserved, then we repent and wish that we had done more; we see that it would have been much better. So the meaning of saying all this is that whatever meditation you do, no matter how much time you do the Simran, all is counted in your devotion. And when you will be able to protect your meditation by yourself, then Master will show you how much wealth you have.

Those who meditate on the Satguru, their anxiety and worry are removed.

Those who do the devotion of their Master, with love and faith for Him, who obey the commandments of the Master, who love the Master so much that they didn't give any place to the worldly things or to the love of the world within themselves – what does Master do for them? Master lovingly pays off all their karmas and He doesn't make them suffer the reaction of any karma, because they were so devoted to Him.

Nanak says, He who meditates on Naam swims across and makes the whole world swim across.

Now Guru Ramdas Ji says that those who do the meditation of Shabd Naam, those who meet God while living and who manifest Master and God within them, those who come to such a Master, they all get liberation. There is no question of His own liberation because He is already liberated when He does all these things. But even if the whole world comes to Him, He can liberate everyone. Kabir Sahib said, "If we could maintain forever the love for the Master which we had on the first day, then what would be the question of our own liberation? We could liberate millions of other souls." Swami Ji Maharaj also said, "The glory of Gurumukh is unique, because Gurumukhs liberate millions."

> **The whole day the manmukh is involved in greed and other things.**
> **In the night he is buried in sleep. All the nine organs of senses make him weak.**

Earlier Guru Ramdas Ji sang the praise of and described the condition of the Gurumukhs, and now He is talking about the manmukhs. He says that manmukhs are always greedy and they are always talking about things other than God; and after working all day long in the world and dealing with worldly people, sleep troubles them; they are controlled by sleep, so they have no time to even think of God. All day long a man goes on working hard in the world; but when he sits for the remembrance of God, he feels as if someone has put a heavy rock on his head.

> **The manmukhs always obey the orders of their spouses, and daily they bring good things to them.**
> **Those who do what they are told by their spouses are impure, foolish, and without any intellect.**

Guru Sahib has not said all of these things only for either man or for woman. The teachings of the Masters are for everyone.

An unchaste person always obeys the orders of the person with whom he is indulging; he always walks in the direction in which he is directed. Such people's masters or teachers are those with whom they indulge. Guru Gobind Singh has said that rare are the disciples of the Master; most people are the disciples of their companions with whom they indulge.

Once Guru Gobind Singh said this, and one disciple replied, "No, Master, that is not true; I am not the disciple of my wife." Guru Gobind Singh laughed and said nothing. After a few days, He told that disciple to bring a unique piece of cloth for Him. That disciple went around the market and found a very good piece of cloth, and he came back to his home thinking that the next morning he would go to the Master and give Him that. When his wife saw that, she asked what it was; he replied that it was the piece for the Master. "I have bought this for Him and I am going to give it to Him tomorrow morning." Now his wife knew what he had said to the Master and she wanted to teach him a lesson; so she said, "Why don't you please give this to me?" He replied, "Well, I have gotten this for my Master." She said,

"Well, is this piece of cloth more dear to you than I am? Don't you love me? You can go and tell the Master that you didn't find any and you will try another time and get another piece of cloth. But you should give this piece to me." Because he loved his wife so much, he couldn't go against her and he gave that piece of cloth to her. The next morning when he came to the Master, he didn't know that his wife was also following him. She had that piece of cloth with her, but he didn't know what was happening. When he came there, Guru Gobind Singh asked him, "Where is the piece of cloth?" He replied, "Master, I tried a lot, but I didn't get it; but I will try again. I will get a piece of cloth for you." As soon as he said that, his wife took out the piece of cloth and said, "Look here, Master, he is not Your disciple. He is my disciple; because he bought this for you, but when I said that I wanted it, he gave it to me." That disciple was very embarrassed. So Kabir Sahib says, "He has become the disciple of his wife, but he says that he is the disciple of the Master."

Those who do things after asking their spouses–
Within them lust is spread.

Whose condition is this, who always obey their companions? Only those who are controlled by lust. Whenever they want to go out of their house, they always ask; if he is a man, he will ask his wife; if she is a wife, she will ask her husband. Those who cannot live without their companions, only they are bothered by lust so much. This is the condition of only those people.

Swami Ji Maharaj says that all those who are the thieves of meditation suffer a lot. Laziness and sleep bother them and they always remain in illusion. They get kicked and knocked by lust and anger and they are drowned in the river of greed. This is the condition of those who are thieves of meditation. Those who stay up in the night and do the meditation, these things don't come near them.

He who walks when the Satguru tells him is the true person–
Better than the best one.

Those who do things according to the instructions of the Master, those who walk according to the orders of the Master – if Master makes him cut grass, he does it – and if he always keeps himself in the commandments of the Master, Guru Sahib says that only such a disciple is good. Because to obey the commandments of the Master is good for his own self.

The women and men are all created by Him.
This is all the play of the Lord.

Now Guru Ramdas Ji says to the Lord, "O Lord, all this is Your play. You have created man and woman and You have made all these things. Only those who have Your grace come to the Master and, obeying His instructions, rise above all these things. Those who do not have your grace and who were not brought into the company of the Master, remain in this world and suffer a lot. Some people get the awareness, whereas others don't."

Nanak says, Everything is Your creation—You are better than the best one.
You are unconcerned, deep, inestimable—how can we appraise you?
Those who have met the Satguru and meditate on You are the fortunate ones.

Now Guru Sahib sings the glory of the Lord. "O Lord, You are *Agam,* unseen, and nobody can know Your glory. Only those who go in the company of the Master and get the instruction of the Master and do the meditation of Shabd Naam, only they get the longing to see You and only they become successful." Those who do the devotion of the Lord with a true heart, they get Him.

The Bani of the Satguru is the form of truth.
One becomes the Bani of the Master.
Those who imitate the Satguru and speak the imperfect Bani are the false ones,
And with their falsehood they fall down.

The first work of the disciple of the Master is to do the meditation of the Naam or Bani given by the Master, to open the veil, and to go within.

If one has not meditated but still competes with the Master, because he is not yet ripened or perfected he falls down.

Guru Sahib explains to us that people imitate those who have become one with God, but they have not yet become one with God. That is why they always fail. That is why we should not imitate the Masters.

In their heart they have one thing—in their head they have something else.
They die in grief, being involved in Maya, the poison.

The Seva of Satguru is pure,
Pure ones do the seva of the Satguru.
In whose heart is deceit or falsehood, they are
separated by the True One Himself.
The true disciples sit at the side of the Master
and serve Him.
The false ones are not found (there), no matter
how much you search.
To whom the words of Satguru are not pleasing
They wander about rejected by God even if
they look good from the outside.
In whose heart there is no love for Him –
How long must these manmukhs be taught!
He who meets the Satguru keeps his own
mind steady;
He keeps to his own.
Nanak says, He makes some meet the
Master and gives them happiness;
And to some who are deceitful, He Himself
separates them.
In whose heart is the wealth of Naam,
God Himself takes care of his affairs.
Their dependence on men ceases as the Lord
sits near them and takes care of their
affairs.
If One has the Creator on His side, He has
everyone on His side.
And all those who have His darshan praise Him.

Kings and emperors, all made by God Almighty,
All come and make prayers in front of such a One.
The glory of a Perfect Master is great; by serving
the great Lord, inestimable happiness is
obtained.
The Perfect Master gives the immutable
donation of the Lord's Naam every day
and it still increases.
The critic who cannot see His greatness is
consumed (punished) by the Lord Himself.
Nanak utters the qualities of the Creator
He has always saved His devotees.
You are the Lord, Inconceivable and Merciful,
Giver and Wise.
I see no one like You.
You are wise and pleasing to me.
Love of the family, all that is seen coming
and going, is passing away;
Those who attach their minds to the things
other than You, the Truth, are collecting
false things and false are their hopes.
Nanak says, Meditate on the True One, as
without meditating on the True One the
ignorant are consumed.
If first the true love is not developed (for
the Master)
Talking afterwards of it is of no use.
The manmukh wanders about halfway; how

can he obtain happiness just by talking?
Those who do not have love for the Satguru
in their hearts come and go from this
world as garbage.
If my Lord the Creator shows His Grace, only
then can one see the Master as Parbrahm.
Then he drinks the nectar of the Shabda of
Master and removes all doubts, illusions
and anxieties.
Day and night he remains happy. Nanak
says, always he sings the praise of the Lord.
He who is called a disciple of the Master rises
up early and meditates on the Naam.
He makes efforts early in the morning; he
bathes in the pool of Nectar.
According to the instructions of the Master
he remembers the Lord,
By which all his sins and faults go away.
Again when the day starts, he sings the
Gurbani (words of Master)
Whether sitting or standing he meditates on
the Naam of the Lord.
He who meditates on my Lord at every
breath and morsel
Such a disciple of Master is liked by the Master.
To whom my Lord is Merciful
Such a disciple of the Master makes others
hear the teachings of the Master.

Nanak asks for the dust of such a disciple of
the Master,
Who himself meditates and makes others
meditate on Naam.
They are a few rare ones who meditate on
you, the True One.
Innumerable are the ones who are benefited
by the devotion of those who remember
You with one heart and mind.
Everyone remembers You but only they are
accepted who are liked the most by You.
Those who eat and dress without serving
the Master are dead and will be reborn
as lepers.
In front of others they speak sweetly, but
within them is poison.
They have deception in their minds and
they get separated from the Master.

5

The Glory of the Disciple

The Seva of Satguru is pure,
Pure ones do the seva of the Satguru.

Mind has misled the soul, and mind is being misled by the organs of senses, and the senses are misled by the pleasures. In this way, everyone is misled.

It is like a princess who was supposed to marry a prince and take her place as the queen. But instead of marrying the prince, she chose to be the companion of a sweeper, and she is not honored. Our soul belongs to Sat Naam, and she has a very high status. But instead of going to Sat Naam, our home, she has chosen to be the companion of the mind. And therefore she has become very dirty.

Mind is wandering here and there in the forest of the worldly pleasures. He is also looking for the time when he will go back to his home, in the same way that our soul is looking forward to going home.

If water is moving or dirty, it is difficult for us to see our image in it. But if it is very clear and pure, and if it is still, then we can easily see our image in that water. In the same way, as long as our mind and soul are dirty we cannot see our image within ourselves, and that is why we need to do more Simran. Simran is the only way of concentrating and purifying mind and soul. The more the mind and soul are purified, the more we will be able to still our minds and see our own Self.

When the King of Balkh Bokhara had the yearning to realize God, he renounced everything. He left his kingdom and sat in a graveyard, doing meditation. After he had left, his son had to host a big feast, at which it was very important for the king to be present. So he came there searching for his father and requested him to come back to the palace and attend that party. The king didn't refuse, and he went with his son. But in order to explain things to him, the king took some *halvah* (very oily food) and he smeared it all over a mirror, so that the mirror was not clear. Then he said, "Look here, son, as this mirror has become dirty because of this delicious food which I just put on here and now we cannot see our faces in it: in the same way, if our soul is not clear enough, we cannot see the image of God."

So for doing the devotion of God, we need to make our minds very pure. Guru Ramdas Ji here says that the service of the Satguru, is very pure and holy, and that only those souls who are holy and pure can do the service and devotion to the Satguru.

Prophet Mohammed said that *momin* or the mouthpiece of God (*gurmukh*) is like the mirror of God. Whatever we are, we see our image in the Master, we see His image according to that. Whatever thoughts we have for the Master, they are reflected back from the Master. And we see the form of the Master in that very reflection.

In whose heart is deceit or falsehood, they are separated by the True One Himself.
The true disciples sit at the side of the Master and serve Him.
The false ones are not found (there), no matter how much you search.

God is Truth, and therefore those who have no untruth within them, who have only truth, what do they do? They come to the Satguru and they do the meditation of Shabd Naam. But those who don't have truth within themselves, even if they somehow come to the Master, after awhile they get misled and they go away.

Hazrat Bahu has said, "No matter if we take the squash to Mecca, still it will not turn into a watermelon." In the same way, no matter how much sugar or sweet things we put into a sour well, still we will not be able to change the taste of the water.

Guru Nanak Sahib said that if we try to explain things to a *manmukh,* even after listening to us, he will go to another place.

The true disciples always obey the Master and lead their lives according to the instructions of the Master; they make their lives true and do meditation.

To whom the words of Satguru are not pleasing
They wander about rejected by God even if they look good from the outside.

Those who don't like the words of the Master, who do not obey the commandments of the Master, are tasteless from within as well as from without. Whatever they do, has no taste; and they are always dry.

In whose heart there is no love for Him—
How long must these manmukhs be taught!

Those who don't have love for God or faith in Him, they wander here and there in the world like madmen.

He who meets the Satguru keeps his own mind steady;
He keeps to his own.

If we want to realize God, first of all we need to go to the Master. And after going to the Master, we need to take care of *our own.* What is our own? Naam, which is present in everybody, is our own. Naam is called our very own, because Naam is the only thing which accompanies us from this world.

Master puts that within the disciples which cannot be stolen. Water cannot dissolve it, fire cannot burn it, and nobody can take it away. Even if the disciple wants to destroy it, he cannot.

Nanak says, He makes some meet the Master and gives them happiness;
And to some who are deceitful, He Himself separates them.

Now Guru Ramdas Ji says that God has kept everything in His hands. There are some people who come to the Masters and obtain the peace of their soul. Whereas some people, those who never have any faith in the Master, do not come to Him or believe in Him.

In whose heart is the wealth of Naam,
God Himself takes care of his affairs.

Master Sawan Singh Ji used to say that if you want to build a house, or some furniture, you can go to a carpenter and tell him to come to your home, and he will make the house. Then if you need something else, you can go to him again and tell him to come. But if you have him living in your home, you can get anything done from him as you want it. It is better to have a carpenter in our house, if we want to make many things, than to have to go and call him daily. In the same way, if we manifest God within us, then everything we need is supplied to us by God, by Master, without our asking; because He sees everything; and once we have manifested Him within ourselves, He will provide all of our needs.

But we, the worldly people, do not even know what to ask from the Master. Except Naam, whatever we ask from Him brings suffering to us. Guru Nanak Sahib said, "Oh Lord, except Naam, whatever we ask from you will bring us suffering. That is why we pray to you to give us the food of Naam so that our hunger may be satisfied."

Their dependence on men ceases as the Lord sits near them and takes care of their affairs.

Those who manifest Naam in their hearts, they do not remain dependent on the world, because they become dependent on God. They have God, their Master, on one side and the world on the other, and they do not understand the world to be as great as God or the Master: the world finds no place in comparison with their Master.

Namdev Ji says, "Oh Lord, if you make us rule over some kingdom, what is our glory? And if you make us beg things from others, going from one door to another, then what are we going to lose?"

If one has the Creator on his side, he has everyone on his side.
And all those who have his darshan praise him.

If God is in favor of you, if Master is in favor of you, then if anyone goes to have the darshan of those Masters whom God and their Masters favor, before having their darshan people may say anything they want to about that Master, but that Master has so much attraction in Him that once they see Him, they become His.

Chattar Das says that we don't know what magic Master performs in His boat. "Those who go and sit in His boat, they never come back, they remain with Him. Sitting in the boat of the Master, all problems, all questions, all disputes of religion and worldly things come to an end." And He says, "Now Hir has met Ranjah." Hir and Ranjah were two great lovers and they are often used by the Masters as symbols of the soul and oversoul. So Chattar Das says that when Hir and Ranjah have been united, then what can the other people do?

Kings and emperors, all made by God Almighty,
All come and make prayers in front of such a One.

Even kings and emperors—no doubt they are also made by the same God—but even they come to have the darshan of the Great Masters. Emperor Akbar, the great king of India, came to see Guru Amardas; that is why Guru Ramdas has written this.

Once Emperor Akbar was out hunting and felt thirsty. He went to a well and met a farmer, who gave him some water to drink. The farmer didn't know that he was the king, but he gave him some water anyway and Akbar was very pleased with him. And he told him later on that he was the Emperor Akbar and if he needed anything anytime, he could come to his palace and he would receive that. That farmer was very honest, and he didn't have any problems. But later there was drought in the country, and the farmer was in a very critical condition financially. So he thought of going to Akbar and asking for some help. When he went there, Emperor Akbar was offering his prayers to God. And after he completed his prayers, he stretched both of his arms facing toward the sky, and it seemed that he was begging something from God. When the farmer saw that, he asked Akbar, "What are you doing?" He replied, "You know that nowadays in this country there is a big drought, and I was begging to God that God might send us some rain, so that we might have peace all over the country." Hearing this, the farmer stepped back and started to leave. So Akbar asked him, "Why did you come? And why are you going back without saying anything?" So the farmer replied, "I came here to ask some help from you, but after coming and seeing you asking things from God, I think that you are not more than a beggar. What is the use of asking help from a beggar? It is better to go to the Lord and ask from Him directly. Why come to you and ask for help from you?"

The glory of a Perfect Master is great; by serving the great Lord, inestimable happiness is obtained.
The Perfect Master gives the immutable donation of the Lord's Naam every day and it still increases.

Now Guru Sahib says that the perfect Masters' glory is also very great and perfect. And the donation of the perfect Naam which They have given to us, that never decreases. Day by day it goes on increasing. If such a disciple manifests that Naam within him, no matter if He gives that wealth of Naam to all the world, still it doesn't decrease in Him; it goes on increasing.

The critic who cannot see His greatness is consumed (punished) by the Lord Himself.

Now He says that God punishes those who, obeying their mind, criticize such Saints. The Saints give the initiation into Naam because they are authorized by God and ordered by the Master. Those who criticize such Master Saints are punished by God.

Nanak utters the qualities of the Creator
He has always saved His devotees.

He glorifies the name of God, because God has always saved the honor of His children. He always protects the children, as the mother takes care of her child. God has created His devotees in every age, and He has saved their honor in every age. He saved devotees like Prahlad and Dhru, and He has always turned His back on the egotist and those who act from anger. Nanak asks for the Grace of such a God.

You are the Lord, Inconceivable and Merciful, Giver and Wise.
I see no one like You.
You are wise and pleasing to me.

Now Guru Ramdas Ji again sings the Glory of the Lord. He says, "Oh Lord, You are the giver, You are the wisest of all, and You are clever. You have come in my heart so much that now I can not leave You. I see no one greater than You."

Love of the family, all that is seen coming and going, is passing away;
Those who attach their minds to the things other than You, the Truth, are collecting false things and false are their hopes.

Now He says, "Oh Lord, this world, this family and everything which I saw as mine before, now looks like somebody else's. Even the body in which I am living now seems like a rented house. Oh Lord, those who, forgetting You, get involved in all these things, they are collecting garbage. None of these things are going to help them, nor go with them, except Your Naam and Your devotion. Everything else will remain here."

Once Prophet Mohammed called all His leading disciples and made them stand in a line. He asked them what possessions they had. When the turn of Hazrat Umar came, he got up and started counting all the things which he owned. He started saying, "I have a son, I have a wife,

I have this and that and all these things." He took something like forty-five minutes to tell all that he had. But when the turn of Hazrat Ali, the very devoted disciple of Prophet Mohammed, came, he stood up and said, "I have only God and You," and went back and sat in his seat. So Prophet Mohammed wanted to show his other disciples that Hazrat Ali was the only one who understood His teachings, because he said that he had only God and the Master.

Nanak says, Meditate on the True One, as without meditating on the True One the ignorant are consumed.

Do the devotion of Almighty Lord; because those who don't do that devotion do not take anything from this world. Nothing will go with us except God and the devotion which we do of Him. All the time which we spend in devotion is counted, and only that wealth of devotion goes with us. Mahatmas tell us that the devotion of the Lord is a very precious wealth.

If first the true love is not developed (for the Master)
Talking afterwards of it is of no use.
The Manmukh wanders about halfway; how can he obtain happiness just by talking?

When the Satguru tells us to do devotion, to do meditation, at that time we do not obey Him. We think that we will do it later on. But when our Master leaves the physical body, then such people repent and weep. But the perfect Masters, those who have done the meditation, and those who have experienced a lot, they tell us that Masters never die. They only change Their body. But those who are attached only to their bodies, they have to repent and they weep. When they don't take advantage of the Master's physical presence, they don't do the devotion, and they don't obey His commandments, they always repent at the end—because they are attached only to His physical body and not that which is working within His body.

Those who say that their Master has died, they should be asked why they became the disciple of such a Master who was involved in birth and death. The real Master, the perfect Master, never dies. No matter if the Master leaves the body right after initiating the disciple; for the disciple, the Master never dies. For him, He changes His body only. The only difference the physical departure of the Master makes is that the disciples do not have the benefit of the physical darshan of the Master. When the Master leaves the physical body, in no case do we change the contemplation or remembrance of the Master. We contemplate on the form of our Master who initiated us, and we remember Him. But if we have any problem in our meditation, if there is any obstacle, or if we need some questions to be answered, we can go to His successor and ask Him, and we can go to His Satsang to receive the benefit of the physical darshan.

One gardener may plant saplings and leave, but the other gardener who works in his place may nourish those saplings. In the same way, one Master may leave the body after initiating the soul, but if the other Master comes and gives the water of Satsang to them, those saplings of the Naam which were planted by the earlier Master, they also sprout and grow very well.

But the new true seeker can be initiated only by the living Master. Guru Sahib says, "The Light is the same, the practices are the same, only the body is changed." But those who have only caught or looked at the physical body of the Master, they remain in confusion. Kabir Sahib said that people have taken the body of the Master as their Master, but they have not realized the real Master, the real Satguru working within Him. And such people remain in illusion and in the cycle of eighty-four lakhs.

Guru Nanak says, "My Satguru lives forever. He never comes, He never goes; He is immortal, and He is present everywhere."

Those who do not have love for the Satguru in their hearts come and go from this world as garbage.
If my Lord the Creator shows His Grace, only then can one see the Master as Parbrahm.

Those who have no love for the Master come in this world and go from this world as refuse. Refuse means "that which is subject to destruction."

Master Sawan Singh Ji used to say that if you cannot meditate enough, at least have complete love and affection for the Master. If you have complete love for the Master, at the time of death, you will be inclined to Him, you will be attached to Him, and you will go to the place where Masters go. If we love the Master, we will definitely go to the Master at the time of our death.

So Guru Ramdas Ji says that on whom God showers His grace, only they see their Master as the Parbrahm or the Almighty Lord.

Then he drinks the nectar of the Shabda of Master and removes all doubts, illusion and anxieties.

Day and night he remains happy. Nanak says, always he sings the praise of the Lord.

Those who understand Satguru as the owner of all and those who always drink the nectar of Naam, they remain happy; they never have periods of dryness and they never have any problems.

He who is called a disciple of the Master rises up early and meditates on the Naam.

The one who is called the disciple of the Master, what does he do? The first thing he does is he gets up in the morning, he sits for his meditation, he connects himself with Naam. *The one who is called a disciple of the Master starts his day with the work of the Master.*

Hazur Maharaj Kirpal used to say, "Leave one hundred urgent works to attend Satsang, and give up one thousand urgent works to meditate." He used to say that as it is necessary for us to give food to our body, in the same way, it is very important for us to give food to our soul – because our soul has been hungry from ages and ages and it needs the food of meditation and Shabd.

He makes efforts early in the morning; he bathes in the pool of Nectar.

First of all we have this physical cover. Inside this physical cover is the astral cover, and within that is the causal cover. The one who is called the disciple of the Master, he should remove all these three covers from his soul and rise above *rajo gun, tamo gun, and sato gun.* He should enter into the Amritsar or pool of nectar, and bathe there.

There is no Amritsar or pool of nectar outside which can remove the dirt of our sins. The real Pool of Nectar is within our body, within our own existence.

The town of Amritsar, which is now in Punjab in India, was started by Guru Ramdas and completed by Guru Arjan Dev, the fifth Guru. It is a copy of the real Amritsar or Pool of Nectar in Daswan Dwar. The architect who was told to make the copy of Amritsar said that he had not seen the lotus of Daswan Dwar, so how could he make it? Guru Sahib gave him special attention and graciously took him up to Daswan Dwar. That dear one requested the Master to allow him to stay there forever, but the Master said, "No, you have to come out, because you have to make the copy of it outside; then I will take you back." So the pool in Amritsar is the copy of the lotus of Daswan Dwar. This outer Amritsar was begun by Guru Ramdas and completed by Guru Arjan Dev, and there was no such place when Guru Amardas was alive. But still Guru Amardas has written that we should bathe in Amritsar—the real Amritsar within the body in which Truth and the true Nectar resides.

So Guru Ramdas Ji says that it is the duty of the disciple to give up laziness and sleep in the morning and get up, and by making efforts, reach this Amritsar and bathe there.

> **According to the instructions of the Master he remembers the Lord,**
> **By which all his sins and faults go away.**

Such a disciple of the Master should read the teachings of the Master daily, and he should reach Amritsar: because by bathing in this Pool of Nectar, all sins and bad habits are removed. By bathing in this Amritsar, one attains the status of Sadh.

> **Again when the day starts, he sings the Gurubani (words of Master)**
> **Whether sitting or standing he meditates on the Naam of the Lord.**

When the day starts he should not waste time. He should go to the Satsang, and at Satsang also he should go on doing His Simran. While he is going to the place of Satsang, he should do Simran. While he is attending Satsang, he should do Simran. And while he is returning from the Satsang, then also he should do Simran. He should go on doing Simran with every single breath and should not waste any time.

> **He who meditates on my Lord at every breath and morsel**
> **Such a disciple of Master is liked by the Master.**

The disciple who does Simran with his every single breath is liked by the Master.

Often I have said that when we sit for meditation, we are sitting at the door of our Master. If the door is not open to us, it means that we are not yet ready to enter His Home. But we should not put any condition to the Master. We should not say that we will sit for meditation only if the door is open to us. We should develop the quality of beggars. It is the work of the beggars to arouse people in the Name of the Lord, and it is the work of the householders to give to them. It is our work to sit for meditation, and it is up to the Master, if He wishes, to open the door for us. If He doesn't wish to, He will not.

To whom my Lord is Merciful
Such a disciple of the Master makes others hear the teachings of the Master.

Those on whom the Lord is gracious and those with whom He is pleased, only such people have the yearning and longing to go to the Master. Only such people like the teachings of the Master.

Nanak asks for the dust of such a disciple of the Master,
Who himself meditates and makes others meditate on Naam.

Now Guru Ramdas Ji says, "I ask for the dust of the feet of such a disciple, because the title of *Sadh* is not a small title. It is a very great title." And He says, "I long for the dust of the feet of such disciples, such Sadhs, who themselves do the meditation of Naam, and who make other people meditate on Naam."

Only those who have experienced the pain of separation know what this pain is like. Only the lovers can tell us how to love. The message of lovers is only for lovers.

I have the pain of love and I am telling this to lovers. I will get healed only by lovers. Without the lovers, the story of the lover cannot be completed. If you think that this is not true, you can fall in love and see.

Lovers do not argue with clever people; they would rather remain quiet than to argue with the wise.

Everybody talks of their own pain. But to whom can Ajaib Singh talk about His pain? He has the pain of love.

The reality is that such a disciple has only love for his Master, and the pain of the love of his Master. By all means and in every way, he sings of the love of his Master. Such a disciple understands all moments and breaths as illegal which he spends without the love and remembrance of the Master.

They are a few rare ones who meditate on you, the True One.

Now Guru Ramdas Ji says, "O Lord, those who meditate on You are very few. Rare are those who are meditating on You. If we search for such people, we will find only few in this world."

Innumerable are the ones who are benefited by the devotion of those who remember You with one heart and mind.
Everyone remembers You but only they are accepted who are liked the most by You.
Those who eat and dress without serving the Master are dead and will be reborn as lepers.

There are few people who do the devotion of the Master; and those who don't do the devotion—those who eat, sleep, and go jolly—they are nowhere counted.

In front of others they speak sweetly, but within them is poison.

When such people come to the Satsang of the Master, they say that they do a lot of meditation and that they are very good in that devotion and so forth. When they come to the Master, they act as though they are His; but when they go out into the world, they become worldly people, because they are always involved there.

They have deception in their minds and they get separated from the Master.

Guru Ramdas has lovingly explained to us what the *gurusikh*, the disciple of the Master, is; what is the glory of the disciple of the Master; and up to which stage the disciple of the Master goes. According to the instructions of Guru Ramdas, we should also try to become disciples of the Master. We should make efforts and reach Daswan Dwar and bathe there, and make our lives successful.

The disaffected One made his servant wear
the black and blue quilt (coat) which was
full of filth and lice.
No one let them sit near. They have fallen
in dirt. The manmukhs came back
having more dirt (than before).
The bemukh (he who has turned away from
the Master) was sent to criticize and
backbite.
There also both of their lives were blackened.
At once all the world heard, "Brothers the
Bemukh and his servant came back after
being beaten up with shoes."
Further he was not allowed to mix with the
Sangat.
So the daughter-in-law and niece came to take
him home.
This world and the world beyond, both are lost,
he cries in hunger and thirst always.
Blessed, blessed is the Lord, the Creator, the
Supreme Being Who Himself caused true
justice to be done.
These words are said by Him Who has created
the whole world.
When the Master (or Lord) is naked and
hungry, how can his servant be satisfied?
If the Master has the things in his home, it

comes in the hands of the servant; how can he get it if there is none in the home?
That seva is difficult (of no use) by doing which the accounts are still seen (by the Lord of Judgement).
Nanak says, Serve the Master or Lord Whose darshan is fruitful, so that no one may ask for the accounts.
Nanak says, after thinking, that all the four Vedas say that whatever the Saints say from their mouth are the true words.
It is well known everywhere.
All are hearing that the foolish ones who criticize the Saint never get any happiness.
They desire the Saints' virtues and are burning in the fire of egoism.
What can those poor ones do if their fate is not good from the very beginning? Those who are killed by the Par Brahm are not undefeated by any one.
Those who have enmity with those who have no enemies get punished when the Lord of Judgement judges.
Those who are cursed because of the Saint wander here and there.
The tree which is cut down from its roots, its branches all dry up.

He who meditates on the Lord, the Master,
his glory is great.
The glory which is given by the perfect Master
does not diminish even a little bit.
The True Lord is in favor of the Satguru;
The people work (against Him) with no results.
He blackens the faces of the critics and the
Creator Himself increases the glory (of the
Master).
As the critic goes on criticizing, the glory of
the Master goes on increasing manifold.
Nanak says, He who has meditated on the
Lord, at His feet the Lord has laid all
the world.
He who mistreats the Satguru is lost in this
world and the world beyond. Every day
he gnashes with his teeth, he emits foam
and in this way he breaks down.
For the sake of Maya he plans every day.
But his former wealth always goes away.
What does he gain, what does he get, who
has the pain of feeling guilty?
He who has enmity with those who have no enmity
takes the sins of the whole world on his head.
He does not get any support here and there.
Who has felt the taste of criticism as the mango.
If he deals with gold it becomes the sand.

If he comes to the refuge of the Master he gets
forgiveness for his past mistakes.
Nanak says, "If he meditates on Naam day
and night by doing the Simran of Lord
all the pains vanish."
You are Truly True and are above all.
Those who meditate on you and serve you,
O True One, their hopes are true.
Within Him is truth, their faces are bright,
they speak the truth and your true strength
is within them.
Those who praise the Gurumukhs and hold the
true sign of Shabd are the devotees.
I sacrifice myself on those who serve the True
One truly.

6

Those Who Have No Enmity

The disaffected One made his servant wear the black and blue quilt (coat) which was full of filth and lice.
No one let them sit near. They have fallen in dirt. The manmukhs came back having more dirt (than before).

In the beginning [of this series of talks] I said that when Guru Amardas started doing His work He was opposed by everyone, especially by the sons of Guru Angad Dev, Bhai Datu and Dasu, who kicked Guru Amardas and said, "You used to be our servant – now you want to become the owner of the throne which belongs to us." They kicked him, but Guru Amardas was so humble that instead of getting upset at them, he massaged their bodies, saying, "Forgive me, because I have this old body; I just have the skeleton and bones and I am afraid that you would have hurt yourselves because you kicked my old body." He was very humble and he didn't get upset at them. Then, when Guru Amardas left everything and came to Goindwal, where He started His work, he was also very much opposed there. There lived a yogi who was performing austerities, and before Guru Amardas came there, he was well known and people went to him. I told you all these things, and I also said that that yogi, with the help of Gondar the shepherd, who was the chief of that village, started opposing Guru Amardas. In those days, Emperor Akbar was ruling over India, and that yogi told Gondar, the chief of that village, "You go to Emperor Akbar, and tell him that Guru Amardas is a fake sadhu; he is not a good man; I am the only good person here, and this person should be thrown out of the country."

In those days, whenever anybody wanted to go to Delhi to meet the Emperor and complain about something, he had to wear a special coat which Emperor Akbar had given to every district. So there was a coat there; but there was only one coat for the district of Punjab, which was very big. Everybody was using the same coat, and nobody wanted to wash it, so it was very dirty; there were many insects and lice in it. It did not belong to anybody; that is why nobody bothered about cleaning it. Gondar didn't want to wear that coat, so he made his servant wear it. And both of them went to Delhi.

But when they reached there, Gondar had to put on the coat because he was going to present himself in front of the Emperor and complain about Guru Amardas. He went to the court and started talking about Guru Amardas, but Emperor Akbar didn't believe him because he had once visited Guru Amardas; he had seen Him, attended His Satsang, and moreover he had taken food from His langar also. So Emperor Akbar knew Guru Amardas very well and he knew that He was a true Sadhu and that all these people were trying to bother him and harass him. So he did not believe Gondar and he kicked him. When he did, Gondar fell down and the place where he fell down was very dirty. So his coat became even more dirty and he was so embarrassed that he would not go back to his home, because he had not been treated well by Emperor Akbar. Word spread that he had been humiliated by Emperor Akbar because he was making false complaints.

When he did return he did not go into the village, because nobody came to welcome him even though he was the chief of the village. So he sat outside waiting for someone to come. Nobody came; but eventually his daughter-in-law and his niece came to receive him. After that, when he returned to his home, he became so sick that even though he felt like eating, he couldn't eat anything. He couldn't put any food in his stomach through his mouth, and he was in such terrible shape that in the end he left the body in a lot of pain.

So all that happened in those times Guru Ramdas has very beautifully pictured in this bani. And he will tell us how all these things happened there.

The bemukh [he who has turned away from the Master]
was sent to criticize and backbite.
There also both of their lives were blackened.

Guru Ramdas Ji says that no one welcomed Gondar the shepherd, and his servant, who went to Delhi to complain about Guru Amardas. Instead of welcoming them, the Emperor blackened their faces and sent them back, saying, "You don't know how to do anything except criticize the true Saints."

At once all the world heard, "Brothers, the bemukh and his servant came back after being beaten up with shoes."

When Emperor Akbar ignored those who went to criticize Guru Amardas, and when he refused to listen to them, when he kicked and humiliated them, then this news was spread all over India: that the critics of Guru Amardas were treated this way by Emperor Akbar. So when they came back, nobody welcomed them in their homes, and nobody talked to them with respect.

Further he was not allowed to mix with the Sangat.
So the daughter-in-law and niece came to take him home.
This world and the world beyond; both are lost, he cries in hunger and thirst always.
Blessed, blessed is the Lord, the Creator, the Supreme Being Who Himself caused true justice to be done.

So Guru Ramdas Ji Maharaj says, "Great is the Lord Who gives always true justice." Because when he came back, he became so sick that he was hungry but he couldn't eat any food. In those days, medical science had not progressed enough that they could feed him intravenously. There was no other means except putting food through the mouth, and he was not able to do that. So he was always hungry.

Guru Sahib says, "Great is the Lord, Who gives the perfect and true justice. Whatever one does, he suffers its reaction according to that justice."

"Those who criticize the Perfect Master, the True One Himself has killed them."
These words are said by Him Who has created the whole world.

Guru Ramdas Ji says, "Masters do not curse anyone. Whatever I am saying, it is not me saying it: it is God Who is manifested within me." He says that critics always repent and suffer for what they have done, and the meditators of Naam always enjoy the meditation they have done.

When the Master (or Lord) is naked and hungry, how can his servant be satisfied?
If the Master has the things in his home, it comes in the

hands of the servant; how can he get it if there is none in the home?

Guru Amardas had meditated very much, He had worked very hard, and he had served his Master. But still, this Perfect Mahatma, Who had done so much meditation, had to leave His original place which was called Kadur Sahib, and had to come and settle in Goindwal; and there also he was very much opposed.

So Guru Ramdas Ji says, "How can those people whose Masters are hungry, be satisfied? Only those whose Masters have something in their home, can be satisfied." Guru Ramdas Ji means to say only this: If the Master has not reached Sach Khand, how can the disciples get any wealth of devotion? How can the disciple think of going to Sach Khand if his Master has not reached there? So that is why the disciple will get only that which the Master has in His Home. Those whose Masters are blind, the disciples also become blind. They always do their own will, and they are always involved in untruths.

Perfect Masters have worked very hard and have spent all Their life in meditating. How can those who have spent their nights meditating criticize others? How can They allow Their disciples to criticize others? Those who have done the meditation know how much they lose if they criticize others. So how can those who have this awareness criticize others?

Swami Ji Maharaj says, "One who meditates on the Shabd, or earns the Shabd, He is the Perfect Master; we become the dust of His feet."

Kabir Sahib says, "Don't ask the caste of the Master; ask about His knowledge. Don't bother about the value of the sheath; learn the value of the sword."

We should read the life of the Master. We should know whether the Master has done any meditation in his life or not. If He has spent years of His life in meditation, then we don't need to ask to which caste He belongs, from which country or religion He comes, because we have to take only Knowledge from Him; we have to take only Naam from Him.

That seva is difficult (of no use) by doing which the accounts are still seen (by the Lord of Judgment).
Nanak says, serve the Master or Lord Whose darshan is fruitful, so that no one may ask for the accounts.

We should not serve anyone if by serving him our accounts will still have to be seen, and we will have to pay. It is better to serve that Master Who has done the meditation of Shabd Naam, because only the seva done for such a Master has worth.

Once Guru Hari Rai was taking a walk with some of his disciples, and they came across a big snake being eaten by ants: he was still alive but he couldn't move and he was in a lot of pain. So the disciples asked, "Master, what is this?" So Guru Hari Rai replied, "This is the result of becoming a false Master. In his past life, he pretended that he was a true Master, and he was teaching people. But in fact he was false, and those people who came to him, looking at others—because they were afraid of other people—this is their condition: they have become ants. He became the snake, and he is paying his karmas by suffering this pain. Because he deceived the disciples, they have come back as ants and they are eating up his body while he is still alive."

Even though Baba Bishan Das had the knowledge of only two Words, He had perfected himself up to the first two planes. He used to say that we should always take a Master after knowing about Him, as we should drink the water after filtering it. If the disciple is a true seeker, he can easily recognize the false Master. When a true seeker comes to a false Master, the false Master at once knows that now a true seeker has come, and he starts running because he is afraid that the true seeker will learn his secret and he will ask for something which he cannot give.

We cannot test anyone if we are still working on the level of mind and the organs of senses. If we are polluted by the dirt of the worldly pleasures, we cannot test anyone. Unless we go within and become pure, we cannot test anyone, we cannot recognize. As long as we are dirty, we cannot know who is True and who is not. If we want to see who is True and who is not, we need to become pure.

Once two pundits, or learned scholars, came to Dadu Sahib, a great Mahatma; they had heard about Dadu Sahib but they had never seen him. They came to him for Initiation, but when they came near His house they saw that a bald man—his head was shaved—was coming out of that house. In India, people believe that if you meet someone like that, it is a bad omen. So those people thought, "We came here to meet the Master to improve our life; but look at this! We have met this man and it's a bad omen; now we will not be able to meet the Master!" They got so upset at that bald man that they hit him on the head, not realizing that it was Dadu Sahib himself, and they asked Him, "Where is the dera of Dadu Sahib?" Dadu Sahib was the abode of peace, and He told them very patiently and lovingly, "This is the dera of Dadu Sahib. You go in and wait and he will come."

Both those pundits went and sat with the Sangat, and waited for Dadu Sahib to come. And after some time, He came, and they saw the same man, whom they had hit on the head; and they were much afraid. They thought, "Now, He will not give us Initiation! We had so much yearning and we came for Initiation, and we insulted Him. He will not even want to talk with us." But when the Satsang was over, Dadu Sahib called them; they were very much afraid, and they apologized. Dadu Sahib was very patient and loving, and he said, "It's all right. You know that if you go to buy a pot, you hit it to make sure that it is good. It's all right that you hit my head to make sure that I am the true Mahatma." So when the Great Masters come into this world, They are the abode of peace, They are very patient and loving, and They don't mind all these things.

If anyone criticizes the Perfect Masters, the Masters do not respond. Instead of getting impatient and upset, They always pray to the Lord, "Oh Lord, if You want to shower grace and have mercy on him, please give him my recognition so that he may know what he is doing.

When Hazur Maharaj Kirpal told me to give Initiation, He told me that His teachings should not remain hidden in the world, and that they should be spread. At that time I presented my shortcomings and lackings, and I told him all about them; but He said, "When the bad man will not stop his bad deeds, why should a good man stop his good deeds?" He told me that I should do this work, and I should not worry about others. When the Masters start Their work, They are very determined. They do Their work with full determination and They don't worry about the criticism or blame which they get from others. They never respond in the same tone.

So Guru Sahib says, "Those who criticize the Beloveds of God, the Beloveds of God do not reply in the same way and they do not lose their quality."

Hazur Maharaj Sawan Singh Ji used to say, "The foolish or mean people always present excuses, and try to prove that they are true. But the wise man always waits, because he is patient and knows that time will tell the truth."

Nanak says, after thinking, that all the four Vedas say that whatever the Saints say from their mouth are the true words.

Now Guru Sahib says that even the four Vedas bear this witness; they also say that whatever words Saints speak, are weighed and are spoken after great understanding. And whatever they speak is true. Whatever they speak is what happens.

It is well known everywhere:
All are hearing that the foolish ones who criticize the Saint never get any happiness.

In this world there are many well-known stories about those people who criticize the Master, and what they got for it. The Guru says that up until now, no one has been benefited by criticizing the Master.

Once some children of *Yadav* caste—into which Lord Krishna was born—came to Rishi Durvasa and made him the butt of a practical joke. There was a boy named Samba, and they tied things on his stomach and disguised him as a pregnant woman. They brought him in front of Durvasa Muni, and said, "You are called Saint and Rishi; tell us what this woman will have: a boy or a girl?" Durvasa Muni knew that they were playing a joke on him, and he tried to tell them that they should not do that, they should go and not bother him. But they didn't stop and they didn't go. Durvasa Muni was very quiet and said, "Sons, don't play jokes on the Saints; it is not good for you. It can bring many bad results." But they still didn't stop. So in the end, Durvasa Muni said, "If you want to know what this woman will bear, I will tell you. She will bear that which will be the means for the destruction of your dynasty." When he said that, they all went back, and when they thought over that statement, later they became very worried because it was obvious that Durvasa Muni had cursed them.

So they went to Lord Krishna, and told him what had happened. Lord Krishna, who had insight, said, "Whatever that Saint has said, that cannot be changed; whatever he has said, will happen. But let us try something. Open this 'lady' up and see what she has." When everything was untied, they found a ball of iron. Lord Krishna told them to file that iron, make dust of it, and put it in the river, so that the iron ball would lose its existence and they would not have to worry about it. But when they did that, that dust eventually settled on the bank of the river and made a very fertile soil in which a special type of grass was grown. That grass had leaves that were very wide and sharp, as if they were swords.

Once it so happened that the Yadavs had a marriage celebration in their dynasty. After doing all the ceremonies, they came to the bank of the river to enjoy, and they drank wine. Eventually, they became so intoxicated that they started fighting with each other, and they used the leaves of that grass as swords. It is said that fifty-six crores of Yadavs were destroyed just because they played a joke on Durvasa Muni.

They desire the Saints' virtues and are burning in the fire of egoism.

When the critics of Saints see that people are coming to the Master and are getting benefit, and that the Masters are getting honor, and are becoming well-known in the world; they don't like that. They are full of ego, and they are burning within with the fire of anger, and they cannot stand that and become jealous.

That yogi who criticized Guru Amardas had this jealousy. He thought, "I know many mantras and other things, and this Guru Amardas is an old man. Why do people go to him and not to me?"

What can those poor ones do if their fate is not good from the very beginning? Those who are killed by the Par Brahm are not undefeated by any one.

Now Guru Ramdas says, "What can those poor people do when it is written in their fate to criticize and do the bad deeds? When God has decided for them that they are supposed to do that work, what can those poor people do if they don't have the grace of God?"

Those who have enmity with those who have no enemies get punished when the Lord of Judgment judges.
Those who are cursed because of the Saint wander here and there.

Masters are without enmity, and those who become Their enemies are sent by God to the Lord of Judgment. And the Lord of Judgment gives them punishment according to their deeds. And those people come in this world again to suffer the reaction of the deeds which they have done in their past life. They continually come and go in this world, and in this way they suffer.

The tree which is cut down from its roots, its branches all dry up.

When the tree is cut down, the branches die of themselves. In the same way, when we become the enemies of those Masters who have no enemies, we lose a lot. The Law applies to everyone: It is not true that the Law doesn't apply to us and that we are special people. The Law applies to everyone; those who criticize the Masters always get pain.

Master Sawan Singh used to say, "Those who like to criticize others cannot give up this bad habit because they are so attached to it."

Guru Nanak says, "There is medicine for every disease but there is no medicine for the critic. God makes him forget himself, and God

Himself makes him wander here and there in births and He makes him come and go in this world."

He who meditates on the Lord, the Master, his glory is great.
The glory which is given by the perfect Master does not diminish even a little bit.

The glory of the disciple who after taking Initiation manifests Naam within him, cannot be diminished by anyone. His Satguru has given him that glory, and nobody else can reduce it.

The True Lord is in favor of the Satguru;
The people work (against Him) with no results.

When the True Lord, the One Who never dies, is in favor of the Master, then no matter what the people of the world may do, they still will never become successful. And in the end, when the people do not get any success, they hold back and repent.

He blackens the faces of the critics and the Creator Himself increases the glory (of the Master).
As the critic goes on criticizing, the glory of the Master goes on increasing manifold.

Now he says that God blackens the face of the critics; day by day He glorifies the Name of the Master and diminishes the glory of His critics.

I have seen this: when Master Sawan Singh was very much opposed by the Akalis, they built a gurdwara right in front of the Dera. They always abused and criticized Master Sawan Singh. But Master Sawan Singh was very gracious and very loving with them, and He would always invite them to come in the langar and have food. He would say, "Brothers, you might want some food to eat because you are doing this work from morning to night. Why don't you come and have some food here?" He was always graciously inviting them to come and eat food in His langar.

Many times the Akalis would invite other Akalis to come and discuss how to work more effectively against Master Sawan Singh. But when the new people would come there and see the Dera right behind the gurdwara, in the evening they would attend the Master's Satsang.

Instead of criticizing the Master, they would become so impressed by Him that they would take Naam, and leave the company of the critics. As the Akalis saw that many people were becoming impressed by Master Sawan Singh, and were even becoming initiates, they decided to move from that place. They turned that gurdwara into a school, which still exists.

Once some four or five hundred Akalis came to test Master Sawan Singh at midnight. They said they were hungry and wanted food to eat. They didn't think that Master Sawan Singh would have enough food in His langar to feed them all and they would be able to humiliate Him and say that He was not a Master. But Master Sawan Singh did not become nervous, although the dear ones in charge became nervous (they had enough food for only forty people). But Master Sawan Singh told them to start cooking food, and said, "Let us distribute whatever we have to them." So they started giving food, everybody was well fed, and in the end, there was still food for forty people.

So Master Sawan Singh fed everyone with love and patience, and they were very impressed to see how Master Sawan Singh was serving them at midnight, when He didn't even have enough food for all these people. Master Sawan Singh told His dear ones that Guru Nanak had been opposed by the Siddhas, who had supernatural powers. Once they removed the teeth from their mouths, and came to Guru Nanak and said, "You are called the Master; feed us. People say whoever comes to you, you feed them well. You see that we don't have any teeth; so feed us some food we can eat." They thought that Guru Nanak would have nothing to feed them because if they were fed with regular food they would not be able to eat it, and they would get one more excuse to criticize Him. But Guru Nanak Sahib didn't become nervous either, and he invented halvah, and gave it to everyone. Halvah is a food which, as most of you know, you don't have to chew; you just swallow it—it is very delicate.

So Master Sawan Singh said, "When the Siddhas came to Guru Nanak, they had supernatural powers, and they removed their teeth and Guru Nanak fed them with halvah. But these poor Akalis do not have any supernatural powers, and they cannot remove their teeth. When Guru Nanak fed His opponents with halvah, can't we feed them with regular food?" So Master Sawan Singh loved them very much and He fed them very well; and they were very impressed.

The dear ones who have gone to Rajasthan know what halvah is; because at least once each trip we make halvah so you will know about it. When the dear old man of Sant Bani Ashram, Baba Gerald, came to Rajasthan, we made halvah. When I asked him how it was, he said, "I don't know anything else, except that it is very easy to swallow!"

> **Nanak says, He who has meditated on the Lord, at His feet the Lord has laid all the world.**

God inspires the souls to come to the Masters Who have done the meditation of Shabd Naam. Souls come and apologize to such Masters. Bheeka Sahib says, "Even if the Master meditates in the world below, still He will be manifested everywhere. People will know about Him, even in the sky."

> **He who mistreats the Satguru is lost in this world and the world beyond. Everyday he gnashes with his teeth, he emits foam and in this way he breaks down.**

Now He says that if anyone treats the Perfect Master badly, his condition is like a dog who foams at the mouth and is not attended by anyone.

> **For the sake of Maya he plans everyday.**
> **But his former wealth always goes away.**

Hazur Maharaj Kirpal Singh Ji used to say, "Who knows what intention people have when they criticize the Master?" Some criticize the Perfect Master because they want more material wealth. But they don't realize that if they criticize Him, the wealth that they already have will go away.

> **What does he gain, what does he get, who has the pain of feeling guilty?**

The habit of our mind is such that when we have made any mistake, he always makes us aware of it. So the Guru says, "The one who feels guilty all day long, how can he earn anything, how can he get anything?"

> **He who has enmity with those who have no enmity takes the sins of the whole world on his head. He does not get any support here and there.**
> **Who has felt the taste of criticism as the mango?**

Because the Masters are without enmity, those who become His enemies have no happiness in this world, and when they leave this world, get no comfort and nobody supports them. Those who feel the taste of criticism as if it were mango juice, may feel that here, but when they leave this world they will not find that taste.

> **If he deals with gold it becomes the sand.**
> **If he comes to the refuge of the Master he gets forgiveness for his past mistakes.**
> **Nanak says, If he meditates on Naam day and night by doing the Simran of Lord all the pains vanish.**

Even if the critic deals in gold, it turns into sand, and he always gets defeated. Whatever work he starts, he never succeeds in it. But if the same critic comes back to the Master, does meditation and remains in the refuge of the Master, Master forgives all his past sins and again puts him on the Path.

> **You are Truly True and are above all.**
> **Those who meditate on you and serve you, O True One, their hopes are true.**
> **Within Him is truth, their faces are bright, they speak the truth and your true strength is within them.**
> **Those who praise the Gurumukhs and hold the true sign of Shabd are the devotees.**
> **I sacrifice myself on those who serve the True One truly.**

Now he comes to the Lord. He says, "Oh Lord, You are the Giver to everyone. You are the Emperor; You are the Donor and You take care of us all. Those who meditate on You, those who remember You, You honor them and give them a place in Your Home." Further he says, "Those who search for God with a true heart, God makes them realize Himself." So that is why, according to the instructions of Guru Sahib, we should also do the meditation of Shabd Naam, and make our lives successful.

Guru Teg Bahadur was killed, in Delhi, because at that time the Emperor Aurangzeb thought that Guru Teg Bahadur was not the True One, but that he himself was the True One. That is why he killed Him, to reduce the glory and name and fame of Guru Teg Bahadur. He thought that if he killed Him, people would forget Him and they would always remember Aurangzeb.

But that is not true; if you go to Delhi now, you can see how people remember that great soul; how people remember Guru Teg Bahadur, and make parshad and sing hymns in praise of God in the place where Guru Teg Bahadur was killed. Even though they are not even sure that this is the exact place where the Guru was killed, still people remember Him there and they sing His glory. Whereas nobody goes to the tomb of Aurangzeb; nobody is even there to take care of the tomb, and it is filthy with bird droppings.

Those who do the devotion of the Lord, their glory cannot be reduced no matter what people do. Even if people take their lives, they cannot reduce the glory of those Masters – because the Lord has honored them and has given them that glory. It may take some time, but always, Those who have done the meditation are glorified.

Those who are kicked by the Perfect Master
(Guru Nanak) are now kicked by the
Satguru (Guru Angad).
Even if they desire very much to be united
with Him, the Creator Himself does not
allow this to happen.
They do not get entrance in the Satsang, the
Master thinks about whether to accept
them or not;
Even those who meet such people are kicked by
the angels of death.
Those who were rejected by the Guru Baba
(Guru Nanak) were also rejected by Guru
Angad.
The Third Guru (Amardas) thought: "What
is in the hands of these poor ones."
The Guru has appointed His Fourth generation
Who has liberated all the sinners and critics.
Whether His son or His disciple, Whosoever
serves Him,
He makes his work accomplished.
Whatever He desires, He obtains; Son, wealth
and riches.
The Lord unites him with Himself and liberates
him.
All the Treasures are in the Satguru, within
whom the Lord resides;

He gets the Perfect Satguru on whose forehead this destiny is written.
Nanak asks for the dust of those disciples of the Master who are beloved friends of the Master.
Those whom He Himself glorifies, at their feet He Himself makes the world bow down.
One would be afraid if anything were done by him (the individual), (but) The Creator Himself expands everything with His own skill.
Behold, O brother, this arena of the True Beloved Hari, who by His Own power makes all bow down.
Hari, The Lord, protects His devotees and He causes the faces of the critics and wicked people to be blackened.
The Glory of the Satguru increases manifold every day.
He Himself makes one praise and do the devotion of the Lord.
O the disciples of Master, meditate on Naam day and night, so that Satguru,
Who is the form of Hari the Creator, may make you dwell in your Own Home.
Understand the Bani of Satguru as the Truth.
O the disciples of Master, Hari the Creator has Himself uttered it from His mouth.
Beloved Hari brightens the face of the

disciples of the Master, and in the world
He makes everyone say, "Victory to the
Master."
Humble Nanak is the servant of Hari.
Hari protects the honor of His servants.
You yourself are the True Lord. You are our True
Emperor.
O Lord, make firm in us the capital of Naam.
We are your traders (of Naam).
We serve the Truth. We deal in true
merchandise. We sing Your qualities.
He who meets the Master, becoming His
servant, the Master beautifies him
with His Shabd.
You are the True Lord, and untraceable.
Only by the Shabd of the Guru may you
be found.
In whose heart there is jealousy for others,
he will never do well.
No one obeys what he says, He stands alone
in the desert and cries.
In whose heart there is back-biting, and
who becomes known as a back-biter—he
loses all that he has achieved.
He who does the untrue back-biting of
others, cannot show his face to others as it
has become black.
In the Kali Yuga this body is the field of
Karma; As one sows, such he will reap.

Justice is not given by mere words. He who eats the poison dies instantaneously.

Brothers, behold the Justice of the True Creator. As one acts, so one receives.

To humble Nanak all this True Understanding has been given. So He speaks of the affairs of the Court of the Lord.

Those who are separated from the Master when the Master is still present, they do not get the place at the door of the Lord.

If any go and join those critics, their faces become flavorless and people spit in their faces.

Those who are cursed by the Master, by the Satguru, are cursed by the world.

Every day they wander here and there. Those who hide from their Master, they wander about sighing.

Their hunger is never satisfied. They constantly cry out in hunger.

No one listens to them. They die gradually.

Those who cannot see the glory of the Satguru, they find no place in this world or the world beyond.

Those who go and join those who are cursed by the Satguru, they lose whatever honor they have left.

Those who are cursed by the Master, they

further become lepers; and those who join them also suffer leprosy.
Don't have the darshan of those who have attached their mind to another love.
There is no remedy against what is written by the Creator Himself.
Nanak says, Meditate on Naam to whom no one can reach.
The Glory of Naam is great. It increases every day.
He who is appointed by the Master while the Master is still in the body, His glory is great.
To Him all the world bows and falls down at His feet.
His fame is spread all the world over.
To Him on whose head the Master has kept His hand,
The divisions and grand divisions of the Creation salute, and He becomes perfect.
The Glory of the Master increases manifold every day, and no one can reach it.
Nanak says, The Lord Himself is the Creator and He Himself protects His Honor.
In the body is a limitless castle in which there are shops.
Whatever business the Gurumukhs do, they collect the things of Hari.

They deal in the wealth of the Naam of
the Lord, and collect the diamonds
(Knowledge of God), and gems (yearning).
Those who search for this wealth outside
their bodies are fools.
They are deluded as the deer is deluded by
the sound.

7

In Search of the Fragrance

Those who are kicked by the Perfect Master [Guru Nanak]
are now kicked by the Satguru [Guru Angad].
Even if they desire very much to be united with Him, The
Creator Himself does not allow this to happen.

Showering a lot of His grace, God has sent us into this world, after making us the leader of the 8,400,000 (eighty-four lakhs) kinds of creatures. If we miss this golden opportunity, then there are many chances that we may again go back in the cycle of eighty-four lakhs births and deaths. Then who knows, maybe we will take birth in such a place where we cannot come to the Path of God even in the state of forgetfulness.

If after reaching Sach Khand we look at the world from above, then we can easily realize that everything is in the hands of God and God Himself is doing everything in this world. That is why there is a great difference between the Saints and the worldly people. The Saints look at the world from above and they do not see even one place where God is not working. We, the worldly people, are the slaves of our mind and senses. That is why we always look at the world from below. And that is why ego and other negative things come and bother us.

So here Guru Ramdas Ji says that those who didn't get the Initiation from Guru Nanak, they came to Guru Angad; but still they were not successful. He means to say that once we have lost the opportunity of getting Initiation, then who knows how many more births we have to take before we come back to the Master and take Initiation.

This truth is known by only those souls who leave, rise above the body and reach Brahmand. Those who become one with God, only they realize this fact. Only they know who is kicked by the Master and who is welcomed by the Master, and who is given Initiation by the Master.

They do not get entrance in the Satsang, The Master thinks about whether to accept them or not;
Even those who meet such people are kicked by the angels of death.

From the Sangat, Master sees and thinks about the dear ones, who is able to get Initiation and who is not able to get Initiation—who is fit for it and who is not. Those who are rejected by the Master, those who are rejected by God, if people go in their company, they also become like them. And they also remain away from the devotion of the Lord. Master used to say that one fish can spoil the whole pond. In the same way, one devotee of the Lord, if he comes into the world, one gurumukh, can liberate many other souls; whereas one person who is obeying his mind can pollute many other people and disturb them.

Many people used to attend Master Sawan Singh's Satsangs, but many of them did not have the yearning to get Naam. Now when I see them, they repent and they say, "No doubt we used to attend the Satsangs of Master Sawan Singh, but still at that time we didn't have any yearning to get Naam."

Those who were rejected by the Guru Baba [Guru Nanak] were also rejected by Guru Angad.
The Third Guru [Amardas] thought: "What is in the hands of these poor ones?"
The Guru has appointed His fourth generation
Who has liberated all the sinners and critics.

Now Guru Ramdas Ji says, "No doubt Guru Amardas showered a lot of His grace on all the souls, but there was nothing in the hands of these poor souls, because they were rejected by God. Even though Guru Amardas showered a lot of His grace on the souls, still they were not able to take any Initiation; they were not able to get any benefit from Him. But with the grace of God, God put a lot of grace and mercy in the fourth Guru [Guru Ramdas, the author of the hymn] and all those who were far from the devotion of the Lord, those who turned away from the Masters and were criticizing Him, they all came and got Naam. And now they are all liberated."

If in our past lives we had met any perfect Master and received Naam from Him, then we would not have come back in this suffering world and taken up this suffering body.

Whether His son or His disciple, Whosoever serves Him,

He makes his work accomplished.

For the Master, the family in which He was born is dear to Him. But all the other dear ones are as dear to Him as His family is. So Guru Ramdas Ji says that no matter if the physical son of the Master does His devotion or the disciple of the Master does His devotion, He always takes care of all his works. He always makes him able to finish all his works; He always connects his soul with Shabd.

Whatever he desires, he obtains: son, wealth, and riches;
The Lord unites him with Himself and liberates him.

Those who do the devotion of the Master, all their works are taken care of and they always succeed in that. And those who have done the devotion of the Lord in their past lives, when such souls come in contact with the Master, it is like dry gun powder coming in contact with fire. As soon as they come in contact with the Master, they get benefit from Him and they go right up.

All the Treasures are in the Satguru, within whom the Lord resides;
He gets the Perfect Satguru on whose forehead this destiny is written.

Satguru is the owner of all things, because God is manifested within Him. But who gets such a perfect Satguru? Only those in whose fate it is written by God.

Nanak asks for the dust of those disciples of the Master who are beloved friends of the Master.

It is a matter of great good fortune. If we have fortune, only then can we get such a Master. But even if we get the disciple of such a Master, that also means that we have very good fortune; it is not an easy thing to meet the disciple of the Master, because within the disciple the Master Himself is residing.

Guru Arjan Dev Ji Maharaj says, "If I meet a disciple of my Master, I may bow down to him and touch his feet. I may tell him about the pain in my heart. And in that way, I may remove all the pain of my heart."

Those whom He Himself glorifies, at their feet He Himself makes the world bow down.

One would be afraid if anything were done by him (the individual), (but) The Creator Himself expands everything with His own skill.

When God has done everything, it means that He has His gracious hand on our head. So why worry about anything, and why be afraid? When God has done everything, He is protecting us. Saints and Mahatmas always remain in the Will of God, and they are never afraid of anyone, because they know that God has put His gracious hand on their head. He says that we should be afraid only if we follow our mind.

Guru Sahib says, "I don't know even one word of mine. Whatever is coming in the Will of God, I am telling that to the people." He says, "Whatever I am speaking, that is not of my own; I am not saying that. Whatever I am telling the people, that is coming from God."

Behold, O brother, this arena of the True Beloved Hari, who by His Own power makes all bow down.
Hari, The Lord, protects His devotees and He causes the faces of the critics and wicked people to be blackened.

This world is like a big field in which God Himself inspires and brings the souls to the Master, and He Himself makes them bow down to the Master. As children are dear to the mother, in the same way, Saints and Masters are dear to God. That is why God performs everything for them.

Guru Gobind Singh says, "When I was ordered by the Lord to come into this world, at that time I didn't want to come into this world, because my surat was attached to His feet, and I didn't want to leave His feet. But God told me, 'I am sending you as my son; and whenever you need me, I will come to protect you.' " The one who is connected with the beloved does not want to suffer the pangs of separation. But the great souls cannot disobey the orders of the Lord. Whenever they are sent, they have to come in the orders of the Lord.

The Glory of the Satguru increases manifold every day.
He Himself makes one praise and do the devotion of the Lord.

The glory of the Satguru increases by leaps and bounds — because They always sing the glory of the Lord.

O the disciples of Master, meditate on Naam day and night, so that Satguru,

Who is the form of Hari the Creator, may make you dwell in your Own Home.

Now Guru Ramdas Ji is saying to the disciples of Guru Amardas, "O my dear ones, O my friends, O the disciples of my beloved Master, do the meditation of Shabd Naam according to the instructions of my Master, Guru Amardas; so that when you do the meditation, He may take you to live in Sach Khand, His real home." The disciple of the Master who manifests Master within Him, connects the disciples with His Master and He never disconnects them.

Understand the Bani of Satguru as the truth.
O the disciples of Master, Hari the Creator has Himself uttered it from His mouth.

Now He says, "Listen, O disciples of my Master: Whatever Master has told you to do, you should do that; because the words of the Master are not ordinary; they are not coming only from Him. Master speaks those words only which God makes Him speak."

Beloved Hari brightens the face of the disciples of the Master, and in the world He makes everyone say, "Victory to the Master."
Humble Nanak is the servant of Hari. Hari protects the honor of His servants.

If the disciples sit together and do the meditation of Shabd Naam, their faces are brightened in the court of the Lord, in Sach Khand, and they are honored there. The servants of the servants are always honored by God, and God always protects them.

Often I have said how much love the disciples of the Master should have for the other disciples of the Master, if they become the real disciples of the Master. When the disciple of the Master meets another disciple of the Master, both of them try to touch the feet of each other and both of them bow down to each other. This is the way the disciple of the Master should meet another disciple of the Master, because this is the way of the devotees. But this path of devotion is very sharp. It is much sharper and much thinner than the edge of a razor. The disciple of the Master who forgets to bow down to the other disciple of the Master, Master will not manifest within him. Those who do not love and respect the other disciples of the Master, Master will never be with them.

You yourself are the True Lord. You are our True Emperor.
O Lord, make firm in us the capital of Naam. We are your traders (of Naam).

Now He says, "O Lord, You are our real Emperor, and we the disciples have come to you as traders to deal in the real merchandise of Naam."

We serve the Truth. We deal in true merchandise. We sing Your qualities.
He who meets the Master, becoming His servant, the Master beautifies him with His Shabd.
You are the True Lord, and untraceable. Only by the Shabd of the Guru may you be found.

"O Lord, You are the True One and the disciples of the Master come into this world to deal in the merchandise of Naam. No doubt You are hidden and nobody can trace You; You are Alakh. But those who take the secret of Naam, those who take Naam initiation from the Master, and those who do the devotion of the Master, those who meditate on Shabd Naam, they trace You and they realize You."

In whose heart there is jealousy for others, he will never do well.
No one obeys what he says, he stands alone in the desert and cries.

In the previous lines, Guru Sahib was teaching the disciples of the Master how they have to love the other disciples of the Master and how they have to meet the other disciples, because we are all children of the Master.

Now He talks about those dear ones who have jealousy for other people, for other dear ones. He says that those who are jealous towards others and have hatred for others, no matter if they go on calling, nobody listens to them. Swami Ji Maharaj used to say that if the Negative Power cannot succeed in playing any of his tricks on the Satsangis, then he tears the Satsangis apart, taking his seat within them, and creates the feeling of disharmony and disunity among them.

In whose heart there is back-biting, and who becomes known as a back-biter—he loses all that he has achieved.

We call them back-biters, who have the habit of back-biting. Even if he is a very good man, even if he does a lot of devotion; if he has this habit of back-biting, then whatever he is doing is nullified, and he loses all the benefit of it.

He who does the untrue back-biting of others, cannot show his face to others as it has become black.
In the Kali Yuga this body is the field of Karma; As one sows, such he will reap.

This body is like a field in which whatever we sow, we will have to reap that. If we do bad karmas with this body, we will have to suffer the reaction of those bad karmas on this body. And if we do good deeds, then we will enjoy the fruit of those good deeds in this body.

Justice is not given by mere words. He who eats the poison dies instantaneously.

No one should think that he will become the great one by reading books and learning many things to talk about and by learning to debate and argue. In that way you will never be able to become the great meditator. No one can expect to survive after eating poison.

Brothers, behold the Justice of the True Creator. As one acts, so one receives.
To humble Nanak all this True Understanding has been given. So He speaks of the affairs of the Court of the Lord.

Now Guru Ramdas Ji says, "Brothers, see, this is the way that God works. If one does good deeds, he gets the fruit of that. And if one does bad deeds, he gets punishment for that. And this is what's happening in the court of the Lord. This is His justice. I am not telling you anything to frighten you, but because God has made me aware of what is happening in His home; and what I have seen there, only that I am telling you. Don't think that I am telling you these things because I want to frighten you."

Once there was a *Punditani,* the wife of a pundit, and her young boy died because a snake bit him in his youth. She was very upset, because her son was her only hope. She started calling God bad names and cursing God. So God appeared there and said, "Look here, I didn't kill your son, a snake has bitten him. I have not done anything in that."

So she started cursing the snake: "Why did you bite my son? Why did you kill him?" So the snake also appeared there and said, "I didn't kill your son. I was born, I was living here even before your son was born. When his time came, he came in front of me and I just bit him and in that way he died. But truly speaking, I should not be blamed for his death. You should blame his time." So she said, "Who brings the time? Who causes the time to happen?" So the snake said, "It all happens when the sun rises and the sun sets. When the sun rises the day begins, and when the sun sets the day ends. And in this way, the time is happening." So that lady started cursing the sun god: "You have become the means of the death of my son," etc. So the sun god appeared and said, "I have nothing to do with this business. I have not killed your son. People do the karmas in my light and when I am away, then also they do the karma. And what they do in their time, they have to suffer and enjoy according to their good and bad karmas. So you should curse the karma of your son, who brought about his death." So then that lady realized that it was maybe because of some karma which her son had done in his past life, that he was dead. So she stopped cursing God, and the snake, and the sun god, etc. She realized that it was his time and it was because of his past karmas that he was bitten by a snake and left the body. So Swami Ji Maharaj also says that whatever karma you have done in this world, you will have to suffer and enjoy the reactions of. Farid Sahib says that whatever karmas you do in this world, they all are seen in the court of the Lord.

Those who are separated from the Master when the Master is still present, they do not get the place at the door of the Lord.
If any go and join those critics, their faces become flavorless and people spit in their faces.

Now He says that if our Master is living, and after taking Initiation from Him, we leave Him and join the critics, God doesn't allow such persons to enter in His court, and He never appreciates them.

Those who are cursed by the Master, by the Satguru, are cursed by the world.
Every day they wander here and there. Those who hide from their Master, they wander about sighing.

Those who leave the Master after taking Initiation from Him, they always go on revolving in a circle. They never get to go in one direction.

And they always are puzzled. Those who leave the Master and join the critics, they do not find support anywhere. And when the angel of death comes, then also they have a very hard time in leaving the body.

Their hunger is never satisfied. They constantly cry out in hunger.
No one listens to them. They die gradually.

Such people's hunger is never satisfied and they always remain in illusion. We leave the Master only when we have unfulfilled desire. We people don't know what we should ask from the Master. Often I say that Master does not give us those things which are not good for us; but when we don't get those things which we desire, then we leave the Master. And when we become the critic of the Master, then our hunger is never satisfied.

In the shop of the Satguru, there is Naam, and Naam is the precious gem. We can get those precious gems from the shop of the Satguru, and we can not get the other useless things. If we go to a shop where they sell only diamonds and pearls, and if we ask for useless things, we will not be able to get them. No matter if we curse that shopkeeper or whatever we do to him, still he will not give us the things which we desire, because he doesn't have them.

Those who cannot see the glory of the Satguru, they find no place in this world or the world beyond.
Those who go and join those who are cursed by the Satguru, they lose whatever honor they have left.

The disciple of the Master who is not pleased by looking at the glory of the Master, he never gets any place to live in this world; and when he goes to the court of the Lord, he is not respected.

Those who join the critics of the Master, they also lose their honor.

Those who are cursed by the Master, they further become lepers; and those who join them also suffer leprosy.
Don't have the darshan of those who have attached their mind to another love.

Those who have criticized the Master and made their soul leprous, we should not go in their company and we should not have their darshan. If we will go in their company, there are many chances that our souls will also get leprosy; we may also get the habit of criticizing.

There is no remedy against what is written by the Creator Himself.
Nanak says, Meditate on Naam to whom no one can reach.

Who doesn't want to do the meditation of Naam and who doesn't want to be a good person? But we can not do anything beyond our efforts; because whatever God has kept within us, only that comes out. Even if we want to do all those things, still we will not be able to do that, if God doesn't want us to do that. So Guru Ramdas Ji says that we all have to do the meditation on Shabd Naam because there is no other practice which can compete with the practice of Shabd Naam.

The soul became the slave of mind only when she disconnected herself from Shabd. And now if we will connect ourself with Shabd, only then will our soul be able to control the mind.

The Glory of Naam is great. It increases every day.
He who is appointed by the Master while the Master is still in the body, His glory is great.
To Him all the world bows and falls down at His feet.
His fame is spread all the world over.

The one who is authorized by the Master to continue the work after He leaves, such a soul gets glorified and everybody in the world sings the praise of such a person. The one who is authorized by the Master, while He is living, to continue His mission, Master Himself is responsible for Him.

To Him on whose head the Master has kept His hand,
The divisions and grand divisions of the Creation salute, and He becomes perfect.

The world will no doubt bow down to such a person. But even Khand and Brahmand will bow down to Him, because the perfect Master has put His perfect, gracious hand on his head, and made Him perfect.

The Glory of the Master increases manifold every day, and no one can reach it.

He has nothing of His own. The glory which He has, in fact, that is the glory of the Master which increases by leaps and bounds. If anyone tries to compete with Him or imitate Him, nobody becomes successful in that; because He has nothing of His own; all that He has is of His Master. Guru Arjan Dev Maharaj says, "What can even millions of hands do against such a person who has Master in His favor?"

Nanak says, "The Lord Himself is the Creator and He Himself protects His Honor."

He has not become a Saint or Master by Himself. God and Master both sat together and decided about Him, and they both have authorized Him. That is why when One is authorized by the Master and God, He has nothing of His own. All that He is doing is of God and Master.

When Kabir Sahib started preaching Naam, the people of the Hindu sect and the Muslim sect opposed Him, and criticized Him. As you know, Kabir Sahib was born in a very low family and he was not very wealthy. So in order to humiliate Him and make Him feel embarrassed, once His critics wrote letters to people everywhere, inviting them to attend the feast which Kabir was hosting. This was a false thing, because Kabir Sahib was not able to afford such a feast. But because His critics wanted Him to face ridicule they invited people from everywhere to Kabir's home. So when all of them appeared there, to have the food and attend that bandhara, Kabir Sahib was very surprised; because He had not invited anyone, and He had nothing in His home to feed them. But when Mata Loi (who used to be with Kabir Sahib) became nervous, Kabir Sahib said, "Don't worry, don't be nervous. Whatever we have, we should start serving that, and if we are blamed, if our honor is lost, we should not worry because it is the honor of the Lord. And if we are glorified and if people sing our praise, then also we should not be excited about it; because it is the glory of God which will be increased. So don't worry, if we lose the honor, then also it makes no difference." It is written in history that Kabir Sahib had only one vessel full of food, a small vessel, from which he ordered Mata Loi to give food to people. And it is said that all the people who came to Kabir's home were fed well. And they liked the food so much that they started appreciating Kabir and praising Him. When they all praised Kabir, He replied, "I did nothing. I had nothing. It is all the grace of my Master. It is all the grace of my God. And I don't know how much grace He has showered on all the people, that everybody is singing the glory of Kabir."

In the body is a limitless castle in which there are shops.
Whatever business the Gurumukhs do, they collect the things of Hari.

They deal in the wealth of the Naam of the Lord, and collect the diamonds (Knowledge of God), and gems (yearning).
Those who search for this wealth outside their bodies are fools.
They are deluded as the deer is deluded by the sound.

This body, our body, is a very beautiful fort. It is a very beautiful palace, in which God has kept many beautiful things. Gurumukhs, those who know the secret of the beauty of the body, go within the body and get many beautiful things. Whereas the other people, the manmukhs, are like that musk deer who doesn't realize that the fragrance he seeks lies within himself. In search of that fragrance, he goes from one place to another, and he doesn't find it. So the manmukhs wander here and there outside in search of truth and peace. They do not get it because the real truth and peace lies within. So Guru Sahib says that without going in the body and searching for the real things in the body, those who go outside are like ghosts who wander from one place to another but get nothing.

He who criticizes the Perfect Satguru becomes
a distressed one in the world.
Hell is horrible and a well of pain. He is
seized and carried there.
No one hears his cries and screams. In distress
he weeps.
He loses all - this world and that. All his
profit and capital is wasted.
He is made into the bull of an oil merchant,
and every day, early in the morning, his
master puts him under the yoke.
The Lord always sees and hears everything.
Nothing is hidden from Him.
What he sows - that he reaps, as one has
sown before.
On whom God showers his Grace, he washes
the feet of the Satguru.
Following the Satguru he crosses over as iron
may float on wood.
Nanak says, Meditate on Naam. Meditating on the Naam of the Lord, one gets
happiness.
Those Gurumukhs who have met the Lord
are the most fortunate ones.
In their hearts light is manifested, and they
are absorbed in Naam, says Nanak.
This body is our temple in which the Light of
the True One is present.

A jewel is hidden in it which is taken out
by some rare Gurumukh servant.
When the Lord who is within all is realized,
then one mingles with the One.
The One is seen, the One is obeyed, the
One is heard with ears.
Nanak says, Praise the Naam and your
seva for the True One will become true
(accepted).
All the happinesses are within those in
whose mind the Lord dwells.
Their faces are brightened in the Court of
the Lord. Everyone goes to see them.
Those who have meditated upon the fearless
Naam have no fear.
Those in whose destiny it is written, they
serve the best Lord.
Those within whose heart the Lord resides,
get the dress of honor in the Court of the
Lord.
They themselves cross with all the family,
and after them they release the whole world.
Nanak says, O Lord, unite me with Him,
seeing Whom I can live.
The place where my Satguru comes and sits
becomes glorious.
Those creatures flourish whom my Satguru
sees.

Blessed, Blessed is the father
Blessed, Blessed is the family
Blessed, Blessed is the mother
Who has given birth to the Master.
Blessed, Blessed is the Master who meditated on Naam.
He Himself got liberation, and He released those who saw Him also.
O Lord, graciously unite me with the Satguru so that I may wash His feet, says Nanak.
The True Satguru is the Perfectly True and Immortal One in whose heart the Lord resides.
The True Satguru is the perfectly True One who has destroyed the poison of lust and anger.
Those who have seen the Perfect Satguru have subdued their mind within.
I am constantly sacrificing myself to the Master to whom I am devoted.
The Gurumukh wins; the manmukhs lose.

8

Humility, Meekness and Love

He who criticizes the Perfect Satguru becomes a distressed one in the world.

This world is like a big forest in which many creatures have come, have lost their home, and are wandering here and there very upset.

Everyone is bothered by the five dacoits: lust, anger, greed, attachment and egoism. But the funny thing is that even though everyone knows that all these five dacoits are plundering them day and night, and there is no happiness with them, still people are letting them plunder them. These five dacoits have destroyed everyone's peace, but still people are allowing them to remain within them. So they are always being conquered by one of them. Someone is conquered by one of the five dacoits and someone is conquered by the other. We obey them because we understand them as our friends. You know that when you obey anger, you are upset. And when we obey greed, then also we are upset. And we already know about lust: when we obey lust, then how upset we are and how our peace is destroyed.

When God sees the people in this world troubled by all these things, He sends Masters into this world to tell people what the things are which are bothering them and where those things reside.

Soul has lost her power over mind ever since she got separated from the Sound Current. We can get our souls connected with the Sound Current only in the human body. Ever since our soul lost its connection with the Sound Current, it has been the slave of the mind, and mind is ruling over her. But in the human body, if we connect our soul with the Sound Current, only then will our soul again start ruling over the mind. For going within the body, the repetition of the Five Sacred

Names given by the Perfect Master is the only means. No matter how many outer practices we do for going within, still they are not good, and they will not help us. They will not make us successful in going within.

Showering a lot of grace, God comes into this world in the human body and gives His own message to the jivas. He comes and tells us, "God, who has sent you into this world, is calling you back. And you can go back to Him through me: Come on; I will take you back to your Home." But Kal (the Negative Power) deludes the souls and makes them resist the Saints, and prevents the souls from following the Masters' teachings.

When Kal met Kabir Sahib, he told Him to give him His secret, and he would not bother His initiates and would let them go to the home of God without any disturbance. But Kabir Sahib knew that Kal was playing a trick on Him, and He was not deceived. Kal tried many other means to know the secret of Kabir Sahib, but Kabir Sahib would not give him the secret. In the end, when all his tricks had failed, Kal said, "Well, now I will give you a very hard time: You will teach people not to eat meat, not to drink wine, to be chaste, etc. And alongside your path, I will start another path in which I will teach people to eat meat, to drink wine, and not to be chaste. And fewer people will be attracted towards Your teachings because they are very difficult to follow. Many more people will come towards the teachings that I will spread. Now the men are eating meat and drinking wine. But seeing them, the women will follow them and even they will start eating meat and drinking wine. In that way, not many souls will come to You and You will not be able to liberate them." And further, Kal said, "I will create many religions in the world. And people who will be caught up in the bounds of the religions will find it very difficult to leave them, even if they want to."

When Kabir Sahib first came in India, there were only two religions there, Muslim and Hindu. Out of both of those religions, there were only a few people who understood and came to Kabir Sahib. The others were against Him. Both religions were against Him.

At that time, Sikander Lodi was the Emperor, and because he was advised to by the Kazis, the Muslim priests, as well as the Hindu priests, he tried his best to kill Kabir Sahib. Kabir Sahib was neither against the Muslims nor against the Hindus. But He was very much against the outer rites and rituals which both of these religions were practicing. And He used to condemn them, in very powerful words.

Once His hands and feet were tied, and He was thrown into the River Ganges. But He did not drown. Once again His body was tied up and He was thrown in front of an intoxicated elephant; but instead of killing Him, the elephant started bowing down to Kabir Sahib. At that time the Kazis were in power: the law was in their hands and they made the decisions. So when the elephant would not step on Kabir Sahib's body, they told the mahout to encourage the elephant to step on Kabir Sahib. Three times Kabir Sahib escaped. They tried three times, but Kabir Sahib escaped all three times. It was a miracle, but the Kazi's mind was not softened. And instead of understanding and appreciating the truth, he became worse. So Kabir Sahib writes in His bani, "What fault have the Masters done that their hands and feet are tied, and they are thrown in front of elephants? The elephant doesn't want to step on the Master. Instead, he is bowing down to Him. But still the Kazi does not understand." We know that in those days there were only two religions where Kabir Sahib was preaching, and both of them were against Him and giving Him a very hard time. Nowadays there are many religions and communities, and most of them are always against the Master.

Master Sawan Singh used to say that the condition of the world is like the condition of the sheep. You know that sheep always follow other sheep. If one sheep leads all the other sheep anywhere on the mountains, they will go there. Wherever the first sheep goes, the others will also follow and they will not realize what they are doing. Suppose the place where the sheep are kept catches fire and someone has mercy on the sheep and tries to bring them out. But if one of the sheep is again trying to enter the place, the others will also follow. They will not realize that they are going to their death.

When Masters come into this world, they do not make us leave our religion. They do not make us leave the society or community in which we are living; because they respect all religions and societies. But the only difference between the teachings of the Masters and the teachings of the religions is that the religions keep us involved in the outer rites and rituals, whereas the teachings of the Masters do not.

Guru Nanak Sahib said that the condition of the manmukhs is like the condition of that woman whose husband is far away in a foreign country, but still she is dressing up. Even though her husband is not with her, still she is dressing up as though he were with her. The manmukhs are doing the devotion of the Lord who is not with them, who is far away from them. In this way, they are not getting any glory in the world. And moreover, their devotion is counted nowhere.

Guru Sahib further says that even if that woman makes a good bed and decorates it with flowers and waits for her beloved, if the beloved doesn't come there and if she is not with him, then what is the use of preparing for that meeting?

When we go to the temples and mosques, and perform the repetitions and austerities, we do not realize God. Our mind becomes restless. And after doing all these things, when we come to the Masters, Masters lovingly tell us that God is nowhere outside, He is within you, and twenty-four hours a day He is always guiding you.

Since our childhood, in whatever religion we are born, we know the teachings of that religion, and we believe only in that religion. So when we come to the Masters, and Masters tell us, "God is within you," we do not try to empty our mind of all of the thoughts which we had since our childhood. Instead of understanding and appreciating the teachings of the Masters, we start criticizing them.

I was born in a Sikh family and I also used to say, "What is the use of following any Master other than Guru Granth Sahib?" But when I went to the feet of Baba Bishan Das, He told me, "This book is not going to help you. Whatever is written in the book, you should *do* that." When I told Baba Bishan Das about the things I thought were written in the Guru Granth Sahib, that there would be no Master after the last Master, and that the book should be taken as the Master—Baba Bishan Das denied that. He said that these things were not written in the book. At that time I was very confused, and I thought, "How is that possible? I have been reading this book since my childhood, and I have been believing that it is written because everybody says so. Why is it that Baba Bishan Das is denying that?" I was not satisfied. I went to Amritsar and brought three copies of Guru Granth Sahib. I had two other friends who were with me. For six months continuously, we read that book and we studied it, and then we realized that the things we were believing to be part of that book were not there. Then we came to Baba Bishan Das and surrendered to Him. We said, "Baba Bishan Das, you are the true one. The things which we were thinking were in the book are not there. And what you have said is true."

What was the thing which I didn't find in the book? That was the thing which most Sikh people are believing: that it is said in the book that the last Master said, "After me there will be no Master; this book will be your Master."

But Baba Bishan Das told us that we could read the book patiently and lovingly, and we wouldn't find these lines in the book. In order to find these lines, we three people worked very hard. But we didn't find those lines. Baba Bishan Das told us that those lines were written *after* Guru Gobind Singh; but they were not included in the Guru Granth Sahib: they were written by somebody else.

When Baba Bishan Das told us that the lines which we were thinking were in the Guru Granth Sahib were not there, He said, "Let us suppose for some time that it is in the book. I will explain to you what that means. Even though it is not the writing of the Master, and somebody else has written that, still if we explain that in its real sense, in its real meaning, then also you will find that it is inspiring you and guiding you towards the Living Master. That couplet says that people say that it is written by Guru Gobind Singh but in fact it is not. It says, 'When the timeless Lord ordered me, then I came into this world and started this Path (the Path of the Masters). Now it is the order of God to all the disciples, that they should take the Guru Granth as their Master. They should take Guru Granth as their Master and they should manifest the body of the Master. Those who have truth in their heart, will definitely get the company of the Master.' "

Baba Bishan Das told us that it was the *Master* saying, "When God ordered Me, I came into this world and started this Path. And now whatever is written in this book, you should take the teachings of this book as your Master." Reading the teachings of this book, you should search for the Living Master, you should search for the Master in the body. Those who have truth in their heart, they will definitely come in the company of the Masters. Every single line of Guru Granth Sahib is inspiring you to go to the Living Master. When you go to the Living Master – if you have truth in your heart, you will get the company of the Master. And when you come in the company of the Master, He will explain to you what all these things mean.

Master Sawan Singh Ji used to say, "The Sikhs have a very great wealth of spirituality in this Guru Granth Sahib. But it is a pity that they don't know what this book is telling them."

We respect Guru Granth Sahib very much and have much love for it. I have been reading Guru Granth Sahib since my childhood, and I have found that in that book it talks about the importance of Satsang, it sings the glory of Naam, and it talks about the Perfect Master. In Guru Granth Sahib nobody is criticized and all the truth is presented as truth.

Guru Arjan Dev compiled the writings of many Mahatmas to make this book. Master Sawan Singh used to say that the emperors of that time thought that this book was criticizing them, and was against their religion. So four times they studied this book just to see whether there was any criticism or not. But they couldn't find any. Still they gave the Masters a very hard time, those who wrote the *banis,* and the Master Guru Arjan Dev who compiled the banis of the great Masters. Master Sawan Singh used to say that in those days when this bani was written and compiled, the Master who did that was tortured. And now also those who are preaching this bani, those who are spreading the teachings of this bani, they are also harassed a lot.

I have seen that when Master Sawan Singh would comment on this bani, then the Sikh people (those who were not initiated, of course) if they would listen to Master Sawan Singh commenting on the bani and realize what the bani was saying, then they would start weeping and they would repent. They would feel very sorry for wasting their time, and they would say that they had been reading the bani for a long time, but up until then they had not understood what the bani was really saying.

So in this bani, Guru Ramdas Ji says that the ones who criticize the Perfect Masters are always troubled in this world.

Hell is horrible and a well of pain. He is seized and carried there.

Those who criticize the Perfect Masters, the angels of death take them to the well in hell.

No one hears his cries and screams. In distress he weeps.

If anyone commits a crime and goes to jail, even if he weeps and begs for help, nobody listens to him. They all give him a beating, saying, "Whatever you have done this time, you will have to suffer for that. And when you are released, next time don't do it." So when the angels of the Lord of Judgment give the critics a hard time, the critics weep and shout aloud. But nobody listens to them. Whatever they have done, they get the punishment for that.

Kabir Sahib says that nobody can erase sins, nobody can say that he has not committed sins. When we commit sins, we may hide them here; but when we are presented in front of the Lord of Judgment, all our sins come out, and we have to confess that we have committed them.

He loses all—this world and that. All his profit and capital is wasted.

The critic has lost. The little bit of whatever he has earned in his life, he has lost that. And moreover, he has made his soul very dirty.

He is made into the bull of an oil merchant, and every day, early in the morning, his master puts him under the yoke.

The critic doesn't get the human body again; he gets the body of the bull of the oil merchant. The oil merchant covers the eyes of the bull, and all day long he makes him go around in a circle to run the machine, to take out the oil. And in that way, without leaving that place he has to travel a lot. He doesn't get any good food to eat or water to drink. Kabir Sahib says, "When you have four feet and the body of an animal; when you don't get any good food to eat; when you don't get anybody's attention; when you are not able to come in the shade by yourself; when you are not able to go in the sunlight by yourself: at that time, how are you going to sing the praise of the Lord and how are you going to do the devotion of the Lord? Your nose and ears will be torn up, you will be roped, and you will always remain a slave of others. At that time, how will you repent for the sins that you have committed? And how will you ask for forgiveness?"

The Lord always sees and hears everything. Nothing is hidden from Him.

God is not unconscious. He is conscious of everything. He knows who is doing good, who is doing bad. And even if we say that we are doing good or doing bad, God is not going to believe us, because He sees everything, crystal clear. He will decide what He wants to give us. He punishes people for their bad deeds and rewards people for their good deeds.

Our mind deludes us so much that we think that God doesn't know anything, and that if we don't criticize people, if we don't find fault with them, God will not be able to know where they are failing and what faults they have. We think that by criticizing them we are making God know people's faults. Those who understand God as unconscious or ignorant are deceiving their own selves. They think that they are deceiving other people, but that is not true: they are really deceiving their own selves.

God knows everything. Even without your telling, He knows everything, and is aware of all things. Masters have so much humility that even though They are great and have no faults in Their own selves, because They don't find faults in others—They are so humble that They always refer to Themselves as having many faults. Kabir Sahib said, "When I went to find a bad man, I couldn't find anyone outside. But when I looked within myself, I saw that I was the worst of all." It doesn't mean that Kabir Sahib was the worst person, that He was a bad person. He was a great Saint. He was the first incarnated Saint in this world and He came in all the four ages. But because of His humility He called Himself bad.

Guru Nanak Sahib said, "My deeds are very low. But since I have taken refuge in You, O Lord, please save my honor." Guru Nanak Sahib also was a great Saint. It doesn't mean that He had really done low deeds: but every single word that He has written expresses His humility.

I have seen both Master Kirpal Singh and Master Sawan Singh many times use very low words to describe themselves, very humble words. Even when Master Sawan Singh was opposed very much and people would put up posters against Him, criticizing Him, He never responded to those posters with criticism. He used to say that if anyone criticizes the Perfect Master—He who has done a lot of meditation, has stayed up in the night, and has worked very hard—He doesn't respond in criticism because He doesn't want to lose His quality.

In His writing, Guru Gobind Singh also shows great humility. He says, "Those who will call me God will go to hell." He says, "I am a low servant of God and have come into this world to see the play of the world." Guru Gobind Singh even said, "After giving up all the doors, after leaving all the homes, now I have come to Your door, and I have caught Your hand. Because I have got hold of Your hand, please save my honor. I am Gobind, Your servant."

God has sent Masters into this world with a lot of humility, a lot of meekness, and a lot of love.

What he sows—that he reaps, as one has sown before.

Whatever we have sown in our past life, we are reaping it here. And whatever we sow here, we will have to reap in our next life. Whatever we do in this lifetime, we will have to suffer the reactions of that in the next lifetime.

On whom God showers his Grace, he washes the feet of the Satguru.

Those on whom God is very merciful and gracious, they come to the Masters. And after coming to the Master, they develop so much love and faith and yearning for the Master, that even if they are told to wash the feet of the Master and drink that water, they will never hesitate to do it, but will understand it as their good fortune to be able to do that.

Many times such souls on whom God is very gracious, become so overcome, so moved by this yearning, that they even move the Master. And Master is compelled to do anything that they want Him to do. Last time when I went to Bombay, one couple came to me and they wanted to wash my feet and drink that water. They brought a silver plate and requested me to let them do that. I folded both of my hands to them and told them, "Please forgive me, don't do that."

When Master Kirpal came to my home, I also wept a lot and I also requested Him to let me wash His feet and drink that water. I told Him, "That water will bring a lot of peace to me; so you should allow me to do that." But He wouldn't let me do that. He didn't let me have that opportunity. And He involved me in talking and in the end He embraced me, and in that way He quenched my thirst.

But Guru Ramdas Ji said that those on whom God is very gracious and merciful, they give up all concern about public shame etc. They come to the Master and forget about those concerns.

Following the Satguru he crosses over as iron may float on wood.

Now Guru Ramdas gives a beautiful example. He says, "If we put a very small lightweight needle on the surface of the water, it will not remain there; it will be drowned. But if we put thousands of tons of iron on wood, it will remain on the surface and can easily cross the water." In the same way, no matter how many bad deeds we have done, how many bad karmas we have, and no matter if we have not improved ourself, if we go in the company of the Masters, we can easily cross this ocean of the world by going in Their company. As the iron remains on the surface and crosses the water after taking the help or going in the company of the wood; in the same way, coming in the company of the Masters, we the sinners can also get liberation.

Nanak says, "Meditate on Naam. Meditating on the Naam of the Lord, one gets happiness."

What should we do? When we have taken initiation from the Satguru, whether we are sitting or standing, sleeping or awake, we should do our Simran. We should collect our scattered thoughts and go within. Outside our mind doesn't let us develop love for the Master, so just go within, just a little bit. Go within just a little bit and you will see how the flames of love are burning there. Now it is very difficult for us to go within, but if, with our efforts and with Master's Grace, if once with all our efforts and His Grace we go within, then it will be very difficult for us to come out.

> **Those Gurumukhs who have met the Lord are the most fortunate ones.**

Fortunate and blessed are those who have got the Perfect Master in this lifetime.

> **"In their hearts light is manifested, and they are absorbed in Naam," says Nanak.**

Master lights the lamp of Shabd Naam within us. And when we meditate, the light goes on increasing and there is light everywhere.

> **This body is our temple in which the Light of the True One is present.**
> **A jewel is hidden in it which is taken out by some rare Gurumukh servant.**

This body is the real temple, real Gurdwara, and to enter in this body is the real and true religious act, because God has kept His light, His Sound, within the body. The Sound will stop ringing within us and the Light will stop burning within us only at the time of our death. From our birth until our death, both Sound and Light remain present within us.

God has kept many other things within the body, all the seen and unseen creation which is created. We can see all that after going within.

If we are in the physical body, we have the contacts of the physical world and we know about the physical world. When we go in the astral, when we start working in the astral body, we come in contact with the astral plane and get to know about the astral world. In the same way, when we start functioning in the causal body, we come in contact with the causal plane, and start to know about the causal plane.

If we are in the physical body, Master also has taken up the physical body and He is sitting in front of us. He answers all our questions. He develops within us the yearning to go within. He tells us about devotion to God and doing the practices. When we withdraw from the physical body and start working in the astral body, Master also appears there in His astral form. And after that when we go in the causal body, Master comes there in His causal body. The form of the Master in the causal plane is the Shabd. When we withdraw from there and go to Parbrahm, Master comes in the form of the pure Shabd. As we go on progressing, as we go on withdrawing from one body and go in another body and as we go on progressing in the inner planes, Master also changes His forms. He appears within us according to our progress.

When we see the position of the Master in the inner planes and how much respect He is getting, what His position is there, only then does the real love for the Master come within us.

When the Lord who is within all is realized, then one mingles with the One.
The One is seen, the One is obeyed, the One is heard with ears.

Why do Masters put emphasis on doing meditation? Because they want you to go within and see the truth of what they are saying. Outside our mind is always deluding us and we always go by the experiences of other people. If a few people say that this Master is not perfect, our faith in that Master is broken. If a few people say that He is a good Master, He is a perfect Master, we start believing in Him. In that way, we are always in this position, up and down. That is why we are never able to make our faith strong enough in the Master.

If we see with our own eyes that there is a horse, even if everyone else in the world says that he is not a horse, he is a bullock, we will not believe them, because we have seen that it is a horse.

So when we manifest Master within and see Him within, only after that do we start seeing Him for what He really is. We start seeing that He is functioning everywhere. Only after that we start to do only His meditation, only His devotion. We start preaching only His Name and we start singing only His glory in the world: because now we know for sure that only He is pervading everywhere and only He is functioning within everybody.

It happened with me also. When I was meditating in 16PS I was not seeing anybody. Many of my relatives were believing that Kirpal Singh had done some magic on me and that is why I was not seeing them and I was doing some things which I should not do. They used to come and say many things against the Master. But I would always tell them lovingly that I have seen only one thing and that is that by repeating the Name of Kirpal Singh many sinners have been liberated. That is why Ajaib Singh says, "You should never leave the support of

Kirpal Singh." When I would tell them this, and they would know that I had so much faith in the Master, then they would leave me alone after feeling a lot of embarrassment.

Once a woman came to me very sympathetically and said, "It seems that some ghost is controlling you. Let me take you to someone who can repeat some mantra and can remove that ghost from within you." I told her lovingly that within me such a Satguru is sitting who can heal people by repeating the mantra, but He is so dear and such a unique one that nobody can control Him.

One evening when I was sitting in the remembrance of Master with tears in my eyes, I came out of the cave and was sitting outside. That woman came with her son and they taunted me and said that nobody else was paying any attention to me. She said, "I can take you for treatment." I told her, "I will not be treated by anyone except Kirpal. For me, I need only one medicine and that is the grace of Master Kirpal. If Kirpal keeps showering grace on me, that is enough for me." When they saw tears in my eyes they were very impressed and they were also moved.

Nanak says, "Praise the Naam and your seva for the True One will become true (accepted)."
All the happinesses are within those in whose mind the Lord dwells.
Their faces are brightened in the Court of the Lord. Everyone goes to see them.

Those who are doing the meditation of Shabd Naam according to the instructions of their Masters, they get all the elixirs. They get all the taste of all the nectars. And you know that the elixir of Naam is the greatest of all. When they have manifested Naam within, they have got all things. So when those who are doing the meditation according to the instructions of their Masters get that elixir within, God keeps many other things within them. God Himself inspires people to come to Him. One who does the meditation, and repeats the Name of the Lord twenty-four hours a day—such a devotee cannot remain hidden.

Those who have meditated upon the fearless Naam have no fear.
Those in whose destiny it is written, they serve the best Lord.

He who meditates according to the instructions of the Master, rising above public shame and the threat of the people, he is never afraid of the people because his Master, his God, is protecting him.

Those within whose heart the Lord resides, get the dress of honor in the Court of the Lord.
They themselves cross with all the family, and after them they release the whole world.

The meditators of Naam are honored in the court of the Lord. God gives them the real respect, the true respect. They themselves get liberation, and moreover, they become the cause of liberation for their generation, for their families. Even if all the people of this world follow them, they can all get liberation.

Master Sawan Singh Ji used to say that one generation of the satsangi gets liberation; and of the satsangi who is doing meditation, a practicing satsangi, many generations get liberation; and many more generations of the Gurumukhs get liberation.

Nanak says, "O Lord, unite me with Him, seeing Whom I can live."

Guru Ramdas Ji requests the Lord, "O Lord, make us meet such a Sadhu, such a Saint, that after meeting Him, we may look at Him and have His darshan. His darshan is our life and we will not be satisfied even after having a lot of His darshan."

The place where my Satguru comes and sits becomes glorious.
Those creatures flourish whom my Satguru sees.

The land where the Masters are born and the land where the Masters go and sit is the blessed one. It is worth worshipping. And the creatures who go to have the darshan of such Masters, they are also most fortunate ones; because when they go to have the darshan of the Masters, their mind gets peace.

Blessed, Blessed is the father, Blessed, Blessed is the family, Blessed, Blessed is the mother Who has given birth to the Master.

Blessed, Blessed is the Master who meditated on Naam.
He Himself got liberation, and He released those who saw Him also.

Blessed is the family in which the Master was born and blessed are the parents who gave birth to such a Master. Blessed is that Master who did the meditation of Shabd Naam after renouncing the worldly pleasures. What does God give to such a Master? God liberates such a Master and gives Him such glory that those who go to have His darshan are also made free in the Court of the Lord.

"O Lord, graciously unite me with the Satguru so that I may wash His feet," says Nanak.
The True Satguru is the Perfectly True and immortal One in whose heart the Lord resides.

Now again He requests the Lord, "O Lord, make us meet such a Satguru, so that we may always remain attached to His feet, and we may always remain in love with Him." Master never dies, He only changes His body; because God is manifested in the Master.

The True Satguru is the perfectly True One who has destroyed the poison of lust and anger.

Satguru is the all-owner; He has controlled lust, anger, greed, attachment, and egoism. He has molded His life in a correct way.

Those who have seen the Perfect Satguru have subdued their mind within.
I am constantly sacrificing myself to the Master to whom I am devoted.
The Gurumukh wins; the manmukhs lose.

He says, I sacrifice myself on my Sat Guru who made my life. Gurumukhs win their body in this life. They utilize their body and go back to their home. The manmukhs always lose in this world. They are always obeying lust, anger and all the passions, and they never utilize their body. Gurumukhs take the profit, whereas the manmukhs even lose their capital.

Those who are graciously united with the
Satguru will meditate on Naam like
the Gurumukhs.
They do whatever pleases the Satguru.
The Perfect Guru will make them dwell
in His House.
Those who have the wealth of Naam
within them,
He will remove all their fear.
Those who are protected by the Lord Himself,
What will the people do against them?
Nanak says, Meditate on the Naam. He
will rescue you in this world and the
world beyond.
The Glory of the Satguru is liked by the
disciples of the Master.
The Lord protects the honor of the Satguru.
It continually increases.
In the mind of the Satguru is the Par Brahm.
The Par Brahm rescues him.
The Lord is the strength and support of
the Satguru.
He makes the whole world bow down to Him.
Those who have seen my Satguru with love,
all their sins are removed.
Their faces are brightened in the court of the
Lord and they get a lot of glory.

Nanak seeks the dust of those disciples who
are my brothers.
I utter and praise the qualities of the True One.
The Glory of the True One is True.
Those who have tasted the true Nectar of the
True One, they remain satisfied.
Only those who know, relish the Nectar of
Hari as a mute person eats the sweets.
Those who have served the Lord through the
Perfect Master, in their mind congratulations are sung.
Within whom there are sores, they know the
pain.
The Lord knows the pangs of separation.
I always sacrifice myself to Him.
O Lord, make me meet my Beloved. I will
roll my head on the ground for them (who
make me meet my Beloved.)
To those disciples who work for the Master,
I am the slave of slaves.
Those who are dyed in the color of the Lord,
their bodies are filled with the color of
the Lord.
Nanak says, Graciously make me meet
the Master, to Whom my head has been
sold.
This body is full of faults. How will it
become pure, O saints?

By purchasing the qualities from the Gurumukhs, one can wash off the filth of egotism.
Those who purchase the Truth with pleasure, their merchandise becomes the True One.
Loss does not befall him to whom the profit of the Lord is pleasing.
Nanak says, They deal in True Merchandise in whose destiny it is written.
Praise the Praiseworthy True One Who is different from the others.
By serving the True One, the True One dwells within, and the True Lord is the Protector.
Those who worship the True One, are united with the True One.
Those who do not serve the True One are manmukhs, and they become ghosts.
They talk nonsense, like those who are intoxicated with drink.
In the Gauri Rag, she who remembers her husband has a good character.
She walks according to the will of the Satguru, and makes the will her ornament.
The true Shabd is her husband whom she always repeats.
As the color of boiled "manjith" (saffron) is dark red,

So she gives her soul to the True One.
She who is in love with the True One, is dyed in the true Color.
Falsehood and deceit do not remain hidden even if they are covered.
Those who are in love with falsehood, glorify it.
Nanak says, The Lord Himself is True, and He Himself showers His Grace.
In the Sat Sangat lies the praise of the Lord;
In the company of Sadhus, the Beloved is met.

9

The Tree Within the Seed

Those who are graciously united with the Satguru will meditate on Naam like the Gurumukhs.

God is an ocean, and the Shabd, the Sound Current, is His wave, and our soul is a drop of that ocean. The drop is water, the wave is also water, and the ocean is also water. When we withdraw our soul from the body and bring it to the eye center, this is the place from where we think, so when we bring our soul there, we come in contact with the Sound Current, or the Shabd which is the wave of the ocean which is God, and our soul climbs that wave and goes back to God. Then our soul realizes that she was not different from the Sound Current, and the Sound Current was not different from God, all three were one and the same thing. And then she realizes that she had lost her control over the mind because she had gotten separated from Shabd. Because she got separated from God, she has become the slave of mind. When the soul gets the human body, and does the devotion of the Lord, withdrawing from all the outer things, and again connects herself with the Shabd, and goes back to God, only then can the soul regain her control over the mind.

The seed of the banyan tree is very small, and the banyan tree itself is a very big plant when it has grown to its extreme. But if someone were to tell us that in this little seed the big banyan tree with its leaves and numerous branches is hidden, we would not believe it. But when we sow that seed in the ground and it comes out of the ground, and when we go on nourishing it, and one day the tree grows big, then we realize that all these things have come out of that little seed.

Guru Sahib tells us that God is in soul, and soul is in God. But we can understand this secret only when we think over the teachings of the Masters—only when we give up our own teachings, our own understandings, and follow the teachings of the Gurumukhs.

Guru Ramdas Ji Marahaj says that when God showers grace on us, first of all He brings us in the company of a perfect Master. And when the Masters shower grace on us, they connect us with Shabd Naam. And when we do the meditation of Shabd Naam, then we are convinced, we get the courage, and we know that we are walking on the true Path.

They do whatever pleases the Satguru.
The Perfect Guru will make them dwell in His House.

If we obey the commandments of the Master and lead our lives according to the instructions of the Master, and do our meditation on Shabd Naam, what does Master give us? Master invites us and welcomes us into Sach Khand. He takes us to our real Home, and gives us great honor.

Those who have the wealth of Naam within them,
He will remove all their fear.

Those within whom Master and Naam get manifested, they do not understand this world as supreme. They understand their Master as supreme.

Ordinarily we do not accept the teachings of the truth, and do not follow the path, because we are afraid of people's opinions, we are afraid of public shame. Many times it happens that when we start doing the devotion, our friends and relatives all taunt us and tell us that this is not our time to do the devotion, this is the time for eating, drinking, and doing the worldly things—and the time for doing the devotion of the Lord is when one gets old. When people are taunted like this, they are intimidated and stop doing their meditation. But Masters say that whatever work we are supposed to do tomorrow, we should do it today, and whatever work we are supposed to do today, we should have done that work in the morning. Kabir Sahib says, "Whatever you are supposed to do tomorrow, you should do it today! You should not postpone your work; who knows when Kal will come and take you away?

Those who are protected by the Lord Himself,
What will the people do against them?

No matter at what time the Masters came in this world, and no matter in what religion they came, they were always opposed and the people of the world left no stone unturned to harass them. But those who have perfect Masters over their head, and those who have the hand of the perfect Masters, God is in their favor. No matter what the worldly people do to harass them, still they cannot do anything, because God is with them.

Nanak says, "Meditate on the Naam. He will rescue you in this world and the world beyond."

We should do the devotion and meditation of Shabd Naam. What reward do we get? If we do the meditation of Shabd Naam, we are honored and praised in this world, and when we leave this world, we go to our home in the court of the Lord.

The Glory of the Satguru is liked by the disciples of the Master.

Only the disciples of the Masters like the glory of the Masters. In the Satsang of day before yesterday I said, "What is the status of the sikh?" The status of the *sikh* or disciple is very high. Only he is called sikh or disciple who reaches Par Brahmand and removes all the three vestures from his soul. If we are the real disciples of the Master and anyone is glorifying our Master, we will listen to him with love and we will appreciate that. For the real disciples of the Master, that meeting is not appreciated where they do not talk about their Lover.

Kabir Sahib says, "Master makes us meet the Sadh, and Sadh inspires us to meet the Master. By obeying both the Master and the Sadh, we can get the knowledge of the Agam Lok."

The Lord protects the honor of the Satguru. It continually increases.
In the mind of the Satguru is the Par Brahm. The Par Brahm rescues Him.

Within the Satguru, God is manifested, and that is why the Satguru always goes on singing the praise of God. And because He always sings the praise of God, God loves him, and He is as dear to God as the child is to the mother. God always protects and takes care of the Master.

When Saints or Mahatmas initiate souls, they take their residence within the initiates in the form of Sound or Shabd; and residing within them, They guide them and help them. Even after realizing and knowing this, if we still go on criticizing others, whom are we criticizing in fact? In fact we are criticizing the Master who is sitting within them. Guru Nanak Sahib says that one calls people good and bad as long as he is involved in the duality. But when he sees within himself the fact that Master is present everywhere, he does not say good or bad, because he has got the knowledge of the Gurumukhs. Guru Sahib says, "Connect yourselves with the Shabd within and then see whom you are criticizing, whether you are criticizing the Master or the other people, and you will know whom you are obeying when you criticize." Mind is the only one whom we obey, and it is he whom we have made our Master, our prophet, and we are always following him, always obeying him. And obeying our mind, we are making friends, we are making enemies. And only because we obey the commandments of our mind, we say, "He is good," or "He is bad."

If you go within a palace which has many mirrors everywhere, you will find your image, your own self, everywhere. In the same way, when we take our soul to Par Brahmand, when we go there, we see our own Self; and after that we start seeing God; we start seeing our Selves everywhere.

The soul who has reached there—she is neither black nor white, neither man, nor woman. The physical body and all these things are below that place; only soul is there.

The Lord is the strength and support of the Satguru.
He makes the whole world bow down to Him.
Those who have seen my Satguru with love, all their sins are removed.

Satguru always receives the strength of God, and always works because of the strength of God. Whatever He has, that all belongs to God. His honor is the honor of God, His glory is the glory of God. And further Guru Ramdas Ji says, "Those who had the darshan of my Master Guru Amardas, the One Who was one with God, all their sins were removed just by having the darshan of my Master."

Guru Nanak says, "Those who have seen or heard about the Master, they never go in the womb of the mother again."

Their faces are brightened in the court of the Lord and they get a lot of glory.
Nanak seeks the dust of those disciples who are my brothers.

Those who have done the meditation of Shabd Naam, God honors them and gives them much respect. And Guru Ramdas says, "I long for the dust of the feet of my friends, the disciples of my Master, who have seen my Master and have followed the instructions of my Master."

I utter and praise the qualities of the True One.
The Glory of the True One is True.
Those who have tasted the true Nectar of the True One, they remain satisfied.
Only those who know, relish the Nectar of Hari as a mute person eats the sweets.

Now Guru Ramdas Ji says, "People come and say, 'Show us your God, show us how God is manifested within you.' But only those who have love and faith in God, and yearning for God, can know how God or the Master is manifested within, and how they can also see God working in Him." Guru Ramdas Ji says, "If you ask a dumb man to describe the taste of the sugar which he has eaten, he will not be able to do that. He has tasted the sugar, but he cannot describe that; he has kept it within." In the same way, the Masters Who have manifested God within Them do not show outwardly how God is manifested within Them; They always keep God hidden within Them. But those who act according to Their instructions, they can easily know how God is manifested within Them.

Those who do the meditation of Shabd Naam, only they can know what the elixir tastes like. Hazur Maharaj Ji used to say, "The work which one man has done, others can also do that."

Those who have served the Lord through the Perfect Master, in their mind congratulations are sung.
Within whom there are sores, they know the pain.

There is one special type of sore which people have on their back. Who can know the pain of that type of sore? Only those who have had that. The one who has climbed the cross, only he knows how much pain he is having. The one who is sitting on the dais, how can he know what pain the one who is crucified is having?

The Lord knows the pangs of separation.
I always sacrifice myself to Him.

Those who have done the meditation, they know how they have to bear the pain, because meditation means we have to fight with our mind. Later on, when we have to deal with mind himself, then we will know how we have to deal with mind. But right now, we are dealing with the organs of senses, and we are loving these things with which we have to fight.

Kabir Sahib says, "The unchaste people have spoiled the name of devotion for the pleasures of their organs of senses; and they have wasted the precious gem of the human body."

Those who have done the meditation, those who have worked very hard, have left the body and gone to Brahmand, ask them how easy or how difficult the meditation is.

Often I have said that the practices of the Path of the Masters seem to be difficult in the beginning, but later on it is not so difficult. Now, it is difficult for us to still our mind and keep it quiet and it is very difficult for us to go within. But if we go on working on it, and if we go within, after that, it will be difficult for us to come out.

O Lord, make me meet my Beloved. I will roll my head on the ground for them (who make me meet my Beloved.)
To those disciples who work for the Master, I am the slave of slaves.

Now Guru Ramdas Ji is making a request to the Lord. He says, "O Lord, make me meet those dear ones, those lovers of my Master, of God, who are doing their meditation day and night, and have become mad in the love of their Master. I am the slave of those dear ones who are singing the praise of my Master day and night."

Those who are dyed in the color of the Lord, their bodies are filled with the color of the Lord.

We get ourselves dyed in the color of those people in whose company we go. He says, "When we go in the company of those who are doing the meditation of Shabd Naam, we also get inspired to do the meditation."

Nanak says, "Graciously make me meet the Master, to Whom my head has been sold."
This body is full of faults. How will it become pure, O Saints?
By purchasing the qualities from the Gurumukhs, one can wash off the filth of egotism.

Now Guru Ramdas Ji first puts a question. He says that this body has become very dirty: It has been polluted sometimes by the dirt of lust, sometimes by the dirt of anger, and sometimes by the dirt of egoism, greed and all the other passions. How can we get all this dirt out of the body; how can we purify this body? Then He Himself responds to the question. He says, "If we get the Perfect Master, and if that Perfect Master showers grace on us and gives us Naam Initiation, and if we meditate on that Naam given to us, only then can we make our body pure and holy."

The soap cannot become dirty even though it has to deal with the dirt; it removes the dirt without itself becoming dirty. In the same way, we cannot pollute the Naam with the dirt of our sins. In fact the Naam removes the sins and makes us pure.

Guru Sahib says, "The Truth never becomes old, and Naam never gets dirty."

Those who purchase the Truth with pleasure, their merchandise becomes the True One.
Loss does not befall him to whom the profit of the Lord is pleasing.

Now He says that those who have done the meditation in this way of the Saints, have never been disappointed. Those who have gone within, have always received the True Happiness. They have never got any disappointment.

We are not stable as long as we do not meditate on the Shabd Naam with love and faith.

Nanak says, "They deal in the True Merchandise in whose destiny it is written."

Who deals in the true merchandise of Naam, and who does the true meditation on Naam? Only those who have been chosen by God from the Eternal Home. And only those in whose fate it has been written by Almighty God that they have to do this work, only they do this.

No one's speed of progress is fixed on this Path. It is not like one's vision will be opened after ten, twenty or thirty years. There is no fixed time on this Path, because it all depends upon our efforts and upon our love. And Master always showers grace, so that is why it all depends on our efforts and the love and faith we have for the Master.

Swami Ji Maharaj says, "When the disciple who has a lot of yearning and longing for God, meets the Perfect Master Who has a knowledge of the Sound Current and Who can initiate him into the Sound Current and take him above, it means that the disciple was already good because he had the longing for God; and when he met the Perfect Master, he became better."

Praise the Praiseworthy True One Who is different from the others.
By serving the True One, the True One dwells within, and the True Lord is the Protector.
Those who worship the True One, are united with the True One.
Those who do not serve the True One are manmukhs, and they become ghosts.

"True" means that which is never destroyed and always remains, that which is permanent. And the Naam of God is the only thing which is the Truth, because the Naam of God is the only thing which will remain forever. So those who do the meditation, those who meditate on the True Naam of God, they go back to God, and they become one with God.

Further, Guru Sahib describes the condition of manmukhs: Manmukhs are those people who do *not* do the devotion of Shabd Naam. They come in this world, they suffer in this world, and they go. Their condition is just like the condition of the ghosts, who do not stay in one place but wander in pain from one place to another.

They talk nonsense, like those who are intoxicated with drink.

God has given this human birth for doing His devotion. But the manmukhs, those who do not do the meditation of Shabd Naam, do not realize that; and they always talk like the drunkards talk after getting so much intoxication. They do not know what they are saying, they do not know what they are supposed to say; they don't even remember what their Master told them, and what is good for them and what is bad for them.

In this bani Guru Sahib explains to us very clearly the qualities of the Gurumukhs and the manmukhs. Mahatamas say all these things so that we may come to the Path of devotion in one way or another.

In the Gauri Rag, she who remembers her husband has a good character.

She walks according to the will of the Satguru, and makes the will her ornament.

What religion is good for us? Only that religion in which we get ourselves connected with God.

The true Shabd is her husband whom she always repeats.
As the color of boiled "manjith" (saffron) is dark red,
So she gives her soul to the True One.

God creates the creation by Shabd, and God dissolves the creation by Shabd. Those who do the meditation on Shabd Naam, they make their lives successful. And when one does the devotion, the meditation of Shabd Naam, for him the colors of the world die out because he is getting the color of Naam.

She who is in love with the True One, is dyed in the true Color.
Falsehood and deceit do not remain hidden even if they are covered.

We can deceive the world, we can deceive our own self, but we can never deceive God, Who is sitting within us. How can we deceive the One who is sitting within us?

Kabir Sahib says, "God is sitting in the window above, and looking at everyone." In whatever way one is doing the devotion of the Lord, he is getting the reward from God in that way. When we put the color of gold on the thing made of brass or copper, and say that it is gold, it will never become gold. We can deceive the people, but when we take it to the jeweler, he will at once tell us that it is not gold. No matter if we go on telling people that we are the True One, we are the Real One; our reality will only be known when we go to the Court of the Lord. We cannot tell God that we are the True Ones; we cannot make Him believe in us. He knows who is true and who is not true. He always accepts the True Ones; whereas the false ones are always rejected.

Those who are in love with falsehood, glorify it.
Nanak says, The Lord Himself is True, and He Himself showers His Grace.

People are in love with garbage, with false things. And because they are in love with the false, and they are attached to the false, they always lie, and they say that they have become one with God. No one can become one with God by reading a few books. When one has to fight with his mind, only then can he know how difficult it is to become one with God.

Guru Nanak Sahib says, "If a woman has never enjoyed with a man, but still she goes on saying that she is married, that she has enjoyed the pleasures; just by talking about the pleasures, she cannot enjoy. Unless she goes to a man, she cannot know what the pleasures are really like. In the same way, if the soul has not left the body, and if the soul has not attached herself to the Shabd, and if still the person goes on saying that he has become one with God, that will never happen. Because by reading books, by talking, no one can become one with God."

In the Sat Sangat lies the praise of the Lord;
In the company of Sadhus, the Beloved is met.

In the Satsang, the importance and the glory of God is explained. And only through the Satsang Masters create within us the longing and yearning to do the devotion of Lord. Masters tell us those things which have become a wall between us and God; they tell us, "Lust, anger, greed, attachment and egotism are deceiving you." And They tell us how to remove all these things.

Once there was a Master Who went to one place for doing Satsang. The next morning, when he was leaving, one greedy man accompanied Him. The people in whose house the Master had stayed the night made three stuffed chapatis for His journey. There came one point when the Mahatma had to go to attend the call of nature. So he told the dear one, "Dear one, you sit here and take care of my things, and I will be back in a few minutes." So this man, because he was greedy, thought, "Let me search through the bags of this Mahatma," because he had heard that the Mahatmas always have a lot of wealth, and he thought of getting some wealth from the Mahatma. So he searched through the bags, but he could not find anything except those three stuffed chapatis. And he was very hungry, and moreover he was greedy; so without asking the permission of the Mahatma, he ate one of those three stuffed chapatis. When the Mahatma came back, He said, "Okay, now let us eat the chapatis which the dear ones have made for us." When the Mahatma opened the bag, He was surprised to find only two stuffed chapatis there because he was told that there were three stuffed chapatis, and he was wondering where the third one had gone. So he asked that dear one, "Tell me, where has the third stuffed chapati gone?" And he replied, "Master, I don't know. I think they gave you only two, and I don't have any knowledge of that third chapati." Master kept quiet, and He said, "It's okay, you eat one and I will eat the other one."

After eating those chapatis, they started walking again; and they came to a river which they had to cross. Mahatma was very confident because He had faith in God and he knew that He would not be drowned. But that dear one was very afraid. Even though he was accompanied by a Perfect Master, still he was afraid. When he went into the river with the Master, he felt as if he was going to drown. So he told the Master, "Master, I am afraid that I am going to be drowned; do something for me. I feel like I am going to die here." So Master said, "God has created us, and He will protect us. So you should remember Him, and request and pray to Him so that He may save you." So when that greedy man did the remembrance of God and prayed to Him, then he was saved; and both the Maser and the greedy one crossed the river without any problem.

When they had crossed the river, the Mahatma thought that now this dear one would speak the Truth because God had showered so much grace on him. So He said, "Dear one, you know that God created you and He showered a lot of grace on you; He saved you from this water. Now you should swear by the same God and tell me who ate that third chapati." And he said, "Master, truly I don't know anything about it. If I had known about it, I would definitely have told you." Master was very patient, and He kept quiet. He said, "Okay." He knew that sooner or later he would come around and speak the Truth; so He did not become impatient.

Again both of them started walking, and they came to one forest which was on fire. Master was confident and he was not afraid to go through that fire. But the greedy man was afraid, and when they came near the fire, the greedy man felt that the fire would burn him up. So he said, "Master, the fire is coming, and we are caught in the fire; there is no way out, so what should we do?" The Master said, "God, Who has created you and has saved you from the water, now if you will again remember Him and pray to Him, he will definitely save you. I have full faith in God, so you do that." So that dear one again remembered God and prayed to Him, and he was saved from the fire also.

When they were saved from the fire, Master thought, "Again God has showered a lot of grace on Him, and now he should realize his mistake and tell the truth. He should admit that he has eaten the third chapati." So He said, "Dear one, you should remember how gracious God is on you. He has been doing so many things for you; He has saved you from the water, and now from the fire. And understanding the same God Who has created you and saved you in both places, feeling His presence, you should swear by Him and tell me about that missing third chapati." So that dear one said, "No, Master, I don't know anything about it. I don't know who ate the chapati; I never ate that." So Master was still very patient, and He said, "It's okay."

Again they started walking; and they came to a dense forest where there were many wild animals. Two tigers were coming towards them. Masters, because They have full faith in God, and they know that everything is in the will of God, are never afraid of any circumstances. So Master was not afraid, but that greedy man was. So he said, "Master, you see those tigers, they are coming toward us and they will kill us and eat us. What should be done?" So Master said, "You should remember God, because God has saved you many times, and He has done a lot for you. If you will remember Him, He will definitely save you. You should have faith in Him, you should be confident." So according to the instructions of the Master, when he did that, when he remembered God and prayed to Him to save him from the tigers, after some time the tigers were not there; they had gone in some other direction.

Now Master thought, "It has been three times that this man has been saved by the grace of God. Now he should realize that God is working everywhere, God knows everything. Now he should not lie anymore, he should tell me the truth." Master wanted him to speak the truth, so that he might get the benefit of his company with the Master. Whenever Masters come in the world, sometimes by telling us stories, sometimes by telling us directly, they always try to make us truthful. That is why they do all these things. So the Master told him, "Look here, dear one. Up till now you should realize how gracious God has been on you. He saved you from the tigers, he didn't let you drown in the water, he saved you from the fire, he gave you many things. So you should swear by God, and tell me about that missing chapati." So he said, "Master, truly if I had known about the chapati, I would have told you in the beginning. Why should I keep telling lies?"

Master said, "Okay." He knew that he would come around. So he did one more thing. He said, "Okay, dear one, it has been a long time that you have been with me, and I would like to give you something. What would you like to have?" He said, "Master, you know that I am very poor, and I would like to have some money, some gold." So he said, "Okay, you collect some pebbles, some stones, and I will turn them into gold." So when he collected some stones, Master turned those stones into gold. He made three piles of it, and said, "God has showered grace on us, and He has given so much wealth. I will take one of these piles, one pile is for you, and the third pile is for him who has eaten that chapati. So now you tell me the truth." So that greedy man at once said, "Yes, Master, this is the truth: I ate that chapati."

Masters know our weakness; that is why They always do things so that we may understand that God is Truth, God is present everywhere, and Masters know everything. And moreover Master knows that only the pure mind, the truthful mind, can do the meditation of Shabd Naam; that is why they always try their best to make us truthful.

By egoism the world is led astray, by misleading
worldly passions.
Only if one meets the Satguru, the gracious Sight
may be cast upon him; otherwise the man-
mukh is in dark blindness.
Nanak says, He Himself unites them with
Him, who have love for the Shabd.
The glory of the Truly True One is great and
is sung by him who is steeped in love for
Him.
Those who meditate on Him with one mind
(with concentration),
Their body never tatters.
Hail, Hail to those, and blessed are those, who
drink the nectar with their tongue.
Those who like in their mind the Truly True
One, are accepted in the True Court.
Blessed, blessed is the birth of those who love
the Truth.
Their faces are brightened by the Truth.
The Sakats (manmukhs) go and bow before
the Master,
But they are not sincere and have falsehood
in their hearts.
When the Master says, "Rise, O my brother,"
they sit down like cranes.
The Satguru resides in the disciples of the

Satguru. Those who are privileged by God are selected by the Master.
The sakats hide before and alter their face and do not mingle with the disciples.
Their lord is not there. The pigs go and eat the dirt.
Though the sakat be fed, yet he vomits poison;
No fellowship should be made with any sakat, as he is rejected by the Creator.
Whose this play is, He makes and watches it.
Nanak remembers the Naam.
The Satguru is an Agam Purush who keeps the Lord in His Heart.
No one can come up to the Satguru on whose side is the Creator.
The sword and armor of the Satguru is the devotion of the Lord,
With which the Negative Power is destroyed.
The Lord Himself is the Protector of the Satguru.
After the Satguru everyone is saved by the Lord.
He who thinks ill of the Perfect Satguru is killed by the Creator Himself.
This is the talk of the Court of the Lord. Nanak has realized this.

Those who remember God while sleeping sing
His praises when they wake up.
Such disciples are rare in the world who
become one with the True Gurumukh.
I sacrifice myself on those who speak the
truth both day and night.
Those who love the True One in body and
mind go to the True Home.
Nanak utters the True Name and always
worships the True One.

10

The Sweet Disease

By egoism the world is led astray, by misleading worldly passions.
Only if one meets the Satguru, the gracious Sight may be cast upon him; otherwise the manmukh is in dark blindness.
Nanak says, He Himself unites them with Him, who have love for the Shabd.

Saints and Mahatmas, beloveds of God, come into this world carrying one and only one mission, and that is of liberating the souls from this world and taking them back to God. And that is why, through the satsangs, they tell us about those obstacles which stand between God and the soul. They not only talk about such things in the satsang, but if we practice the Path—if we get initiated into the Path of the Surat Shabd and if we meditate according to the instruction of the Masters—they help us from within and without. From outside, through their satsangs they tell us our shortcomings and the remedies for them; and after we get encouragement from Them through the satsangs, when we go within They are there in the form of the Shabd. And that form of the Master helps us within and takes our soul back to God. The more we make our mind pure, and the more we do Simran with our purer mind, the more our mind and soul will get concentrated.

When our mind and soul get more concentrated, become still at the eye center and stop wandering here and there, then we cross the stars, sun and moon, and after that we come to the Radiant Form of the Master.

Now, when the Form of the Master first appears, people get upset and complain that the Form doesn't stay there: they say that it comes and goes; they see the Form of the Master only for some time and then it disappears. But that is not true. The Form of the Master doesn't go anywhere, it is always present there at the eye center. It is something like this: We cannot see our image in moving, rippling water, and if the water is dirty we cannot see our face no matter what we do. But if we clean the water and it remains stable at one place, then we can see our face very clearly. In the same way, as long as our soul and mind are not pure, the mirror of our soul is not clear and we cannot see the image of God in it. When we concentrate our mind and soul and make them both pure enough, then we will see the image of the Master very clearly, and it will always remain there.

When we are in the physical body, Master is in front of us in His physical body. When we go to the first plane, *Sahans dal Kanwal,* there the Form of the Master is Light. And when we go to Par Brahm, there the Form of the Master is Shabd. We can know about the perfection and reality of the Master only when we go to Par Brahm. Only then can we know the glory of the Master, the importance of the Master, and what mission He has brought into this world.

If a child goes to school, and on the very first day the teacher tells him that he will have to study for sixteen or seventeen years to graduate, and how many big books he will have to read and how many courses he will have to take, the child will get nervous and he will not be able to learn even the studies of the first grade. So the teachers don't reveal all their competence to the child on the very first day. They pretend they know only the teachings of the first grade, because they want to teach the child. They don't tell the child that they know a lot. As the child grows, he goes on to second and third grade and the teacher reveals more of his competence to him. By the time he goes to high school, the student has learned a lot and the teacher tells him more about his competence, and the student starts having respect and appreciation for him and begins to realize how much the teacher knows. By the time he graduates from college and begins work for the master's degree, the teacher reveals all his competence and the student can grasp everything. Then the teacher reveals everything and doesn't withhold anything. Because the child studied gradually, he was not nervous on the first day. And by the time people get the master's degree, then they don't remember how they had passed the lower grades. They don't even remember that they have spent so many years. But if in the beginning you tell them that they will have to come to school daily for sixteen or seventeen years, nobody will want to do that.

In the same way, if on the very first day Master reveals all His competence to you, you will be very nervous and you will not be able to progress. As you go on progressing in meditation Master also goes on revealing His competence to you. When we are in the physical body, Master also has a physical body and in it He responds to all our questions. And outwardly He helps us and He inspires and encourages us to go within.

When we go in the astral plane and get the astral body, Master comes there in His astral body and He responds to our questions and guides us to the higher planes above.

And when we go in the causal plane and start working through the causal body, Master also takes up His causal body and there also He responds to all our questions.

After that, when our soul goes to Par Brahm in the Daswan Dwar and comes in the form of complete Light, then Master's Form is the Pure Shabd. And then that Shabd Form of the Master takes us above.

So Master teaches us gradually. When we are in the physical body He works through His physical body and teaches us. As we go on increasing our yearning for meditation, as we go on progressing in meditation, Master begins to reveal His competence. So it is said that unless you go within you cannot know how very important the Master is, or what His mission is. You cannot know about the perfection of the Master unless you reach Daswan Dwar.

So long as Saints are working in the physical body, they never say, "I am your Master." They never say, "Take me as your Master." They say, "You can consider me as your brother, your younger brother or your older brother, or your friend, or your teacher. Whatever you want to call me, you can say that. But go within. And once you have gone within and have seen what my real Form is there, after that you can call me whatever name you want."

After going within, no doubts remain. Outside, you don't know when your mind is going to deceive you. The condition of our mind outside is that if a few people come and tell you, "He is a Perfect Master," you will start believing in Him, and if a few people come and tell you that He is not a Perfect Master, then your faith in Him will be shaken and you will no longer believe in Him.

Masters do not mean to involve us in meditation for all our life. They do not mean that we should go on suffering pain in meditation for all our life. They say, "Meditate correctly, abstaining from all the things which we tell you to abstain from, and keep your love and faith in the Master. If you do this just for some time, you can become successful."

The first step is to develop love for the Master. When you have love for the Master, only then are you able to progress within. Masters are not hungry for the love of their disciples; the mirror doesn't say, "Come and look at your face in me." If you want to see what your face looks like, you need to go to the mirror. The mirror is not inviting you. In the same way, Masters are not hungry for your love, because they are already in love with Their Master. But unless the disciple has love for the Master he cannot go even a little bit within.

Masters work in two ways. On one side they have become one with God and they are bringing the message of God and giving it to the people. On the other side, because they are in the world they are connected with the world and they inspire the people to go within and get connected with God.

We know that when we have love for the Master, whenever Masters give us Their darshan, we never even remember our body—we don't have any awareness of our body—and if we are sitting in the satsang with complete love and full devotion for the Master, then we are not even aware of the time. We don't even know when the hour or hour and a half of the satsang has passed because we are so absorbed in the darshan of the Master. We can get this absorbed in the Master only if we have love for Him.

There is no better austerity in the world than to carry the Form of the Master within at all times and to always have the sweet remembrance of Master. And there is no better repetition than doing the Simran of the Master all day long.

Masters tell us about the obstacles or hindrances which stand between us and God. What are those obstacles? Egoism is one. What is egoism? Egoism is when we say, "This is my community," "This is my religion," "This is my family," "I am a learned man"—anything in which the sense of I-hood comes, that is counted as egoism. Those on whom God showers His grace, He brings them to a Master, and Master graciously shows them the Path. And if those dear ones start practicing the Path which the Master has shown, they can easily remove this obstacle. When we buy a ticket and sit in a train, then it is the responsibility of the railroad to take us to our destination. We are no longer responsible for our journey. In the same way, when we collect our scattered attention with the help of Simran and bring our attention to the eye center, then it becomes the responsibility of the Master to take us up.

The glory of the Truly True One is great and is sung by him who is steeped in love for Him.
Those who meditate on Him with one mind (with concentration),
Their body never tatters.

Now Guru Ramdas Ji sings the glory of doing the devotion of the Lord. Because we have only one mind, we can do only one thing at a time.

Either we can do the devotion of the Lord, or we can indulge in worldly pleasures.

> **Hail, Hail to those, and blessed are those, who drink the nectar with their tongue.**
> **Those who like in their mind the Truly True One, are accepted in the True Court.**
> **Blessed, blessed is the birth of those who love the Truth.**
> **Their faces are brightened by the Truth.**

Blessed are the people who are engaged in the devotion of the Lord day and night, who are singing the glory of the Lord day and night, and who are doing His Simran. Such people are honored in the Court of the Lord; they are given a special place to reside there and they are very much respected by Him. If there is anything precious, any greatest wealth, anything which will go with us when we will leave this world, it is the Naam of the Lord.

> **The Sakats (manmukhs) go and bow before the Master,**
> **But they are not sincere and have falsehood in their hearts.**

There are two kinds of people: *gurumukhs* and *manmukhs.* The Muslims call those who do the devotion of the Lord *momins,* and those who don't devote themselves to God, they call *kafirs.* Master Sawan Singh Ji used to say, "To the Masters numerous kinds of people come. Some people come just out of curiosity to see what is happening there; some people come because they see that other people are going; some people come only to steal things and enjoy. But some dear souls come who have a yearning for God." Those who come to the Masters only out of curiosity never get inclined to the Masters and to the devotion. They are worldly people, and no matter how much time they spend in satsang, still they can never come to the Path of devotion. No matter if you put a stone in water for ten days or for millions of years still not a drop of water will enter into the stone. It is the same with the *sakats* or worldly people: no matter how much time they sit in the satsang of the Masters, no matter how many years they spend with the Masters, still they are like a stone which does not absorb any water.

That is why Hazrat Bahu said that we should not go in the company of such people, we should not get attached to them and thus bring a bad name to our generation. No matter if you pick a squash and take it to Mecca, still it will not turn into a watermelon. No matter if you put hundreds of tons of sugar in a sour well, still you cannot turn the taste of the water. Such people may boast that they have spent so much time with the Masters and they have done this and that with the Master; but still they are far away from the Master. Master Kirpal used to say that the people who are around the Master are bloodsuckers; and Master Sawan Singh used to say this very often too.

> **When the Master says, "Rise, O my brother," they sit down like cranes.**
> **The Satguru resides in the disciples of the Satguru. Those who are privileged by God are selected by the Master.**

The Master knows everything: who are the loving souls, who are the true souls, and who are sitting in meditation like cranes—they just close their eyes and pretend they are doing meditation, but in their mind, they are thinking about something else. So when the Master puts the disciple to the test, he knows who is the true one and who is not. Mahatma Charan Das says that the crane has a beautiful white body similar to the swan's body, and he is standing on one foot pretending to do the devotion of the Lord—but how can he realize God when he is having the desire of catching fish?

Mahatmas are very wise and clever, and they know how to put the dear ones to the test, and they know who is the true soul and who is not. So whenever they want to test anyone, they just stop giving honor to him and they tell him to do something which he doesn't want to do. Those who are not true ones get upset, and that's all. On the other side, within the true disciples Master Himself resides. And that is why it is not difficult for the Master to separate the true souls from the false.

Once there was one disciple of Guru Arjan Dev whose name was Mana, and he refused to work in the langar, even though he came to get food before anybody else. But he was not interested in doing seva. So those dear ones who were working hard were upset with him. Whenever they would tell him to do anything, he would say, "I will not obey my equals. If Master will order me, only then will I do this work." The dear ones were tired of him, so they complained to the Master.

So the Master called him and said, "Well, like others, you also have the right to eat from the langar. But like others, you should also work in the langar." He said, "Master, no. First of all, I don't want to do what the other people, my equals, want me to do. But if you will give me any order, I will definitely carry it out. But don't tell me to work in the langar."

So Guru Arjan Dev Ji told him, "Okay, if you don't want to work in the langar and if you say that you will obey my orders, go into the forest, collect some wood, light a fire with it, and burn your body in that fire." Guru Arjan Dev knew that he would not do that; but he was putting him to the test.

Mana went to the forest and started obeying the orders of the Master: he collected some wood and burned it—but he was afraid of the fire. He went around the fire many times, thinking how to enter the fire, but he was very much afraid. After some time he said, "Well, I can't obey this order." So he left off that idea of obeying the Master's orders.

A thief came there who was being chased by the police because he had robbed things from some big trader's house. He asked Mana what he was doing there in the forest and why there was a fire. So Mana told him his story.

The thief was very much impressed, and he said, "Do you want to exchange the word of the Master for this wealth? You give me the order of your Master and I will carry that out, and you take the wealth which I have robbed." Mana became very happy, thinking he was getting a good deal. So Mana gave him the order to burn himself in the fire and he took the wealth from the thief. That thief at once jumped into the fire because he knew that the police would come and take him to prison. In order to escape from the police he preferred to die, so he jumped into the fire and his soul was liberated by Guru Arjan Dev because he was obeying the orders of the Master.

But when the police arrived and found Mana, they recovered all the wealth which was stolen. They took Mana into custody, thinking that he was the thief, and there he was punished a lot. So, our mind may say that we will not obey the orders of others—if Master directly gives us the order, only then will we obey. But our mind is such a tricky thing that he will not let us obey even the direct orders of the Master.

Whenever Masters want to test anyone, they give them some work to do which they are not able to do and in which they fail, and then it becomes very obvious that they were not true disciples.

The sakats hide before and alter their face and do not mingle with the disciples.
Their lord is not there. The pigs go and eat the dirt.

Such people cannot sit with the dear ones, and they cannot talk about meditation. When the dear ones are doing seva such people will go and sit for meditation. And there, the mind will give them a hard time and they will not be able to meditate. So they will neither do the seva nor will they do the meditation. And then they will go in one corner, find some other people like themselves, form a party, and start criticizing and backbiting others. And in that way, instead of purifying the soul—the purpose for which they came to the Master—they will defile, they will *pollute* their soul more than they could purify it by attending the satsang and doing a little bit of meditation.

Guru Sahib says, "As the pig is attracted by the dirt—as soon as he sees any dirt he goes and eats there—in the same way, those who don't obey the orders of the Master are attracted by occasions where they can criticize and backbite." Master Sawan Singh Ji used to say that when we have come to the satsang, either we should do seva or we should meditate or we should attend satsang. We should not do anything else besides these three things.

Though the sakat be fed, yet he vomits poison;
No fellowship should be made with any sakat, as he is rejected by the Creator.

He is called a sakat who has no love and affection for God and the Master, and whose heart is very black and dirty. His condition is like the snake: no matter how much milk you give a snake, as soon as the snake drinks it, it will turn into poison. In the same way, no matter how much grace is showered on such sakats, they will not change for the better, and no matter how much you tell them, still they will continue doing criticism and backbiting and other bad things. So Guru Ramdas says, "Don't go in their company, because they are rejected by God." Kabir Sahib said, "You should never go in the company of sakats. Even if you see them coming from afar, you should run away. Don't even look at them. Because, even if we don't talk to them, still, if they touch us we can get stained."

Whose this play is, He makes and watches it.
Nanak remembers the Naam.

God has kept everything in His hands. He decides whom He has to bring to Him, whom He has to unite with Him, and whom He still has to keep in the state of forgetfulness, wandering here and there. Those who are chosen by God for union with Him, He makes them good people. "He makes them good people" means that He makes them do the meditation of Shabd Naam; whereas those people who are not chosen by God for union with Him, they are made bad people by God and they are made to spend their time involved in criticizing, backbiting and other bad habits. And because of those bad habits they never come to the Masters and never get united with God.*

Guru Sahib says, "Oh Lord, You Yourself have created the true ones and the false ones, and You Yourself know who are the true ones and the false ones. That is why You accept only the true and reject the false; You keep them in illusion and make them wander here and there in the creation."

The Satguru is an Agam Purush who keeps the Lord in His Heart.
No one can come up to the Satguru on whose side is the Creator.

Now Guru Ramdas Ji says, "Satguru is Agam Purush, He is competent, no one can compete with Him, because God is manifested within Him and no one can reach to Him."

The sword and armor of the Satguru is the devotion of the Lord,
With which the Negative Power is destroyed.

What sword does Master have, what weapon does Master use in liberating the souls? The Master has the sword of the devotion of the Lord, and He's wearing the armor of the Shabd Naam. In the olden days, when people fought in battles using swords, they wore armor made of chains and iron to protect themselves. So here Guru Sahib says that Satguru has the sword of devotion and He is wearing the armor of Shabd Naam. And using His weapons, He's fighting with His enemy, the Negative Power, and He's rescuing the souls.

The Lord Himself is the Protector of the Satguru.
After the Satguru everyone is saved by the Lord.

As long as the child remains in the lap of the mother, he's comfortable because the mother is responsible for his bathing, his eating; she knows at what time she has to do what; and she takes every care of her child. But when the child gets down from the lap, she doesn't care so much about him. In the same way, as long as we remain in the lap of the Master, He worries about us, and He takes good care of us. God protects the Master, because God works through the Master, and God is worried about the Master; that is why as long as we remain in the lap

* EDITOR'S NOTE: Here the Master wishes to emphasize the power of God, so He speaks in this way. But it is part of the paradox that is the universe. It is absolutely true that

of the Master and understand ourselves as the instrument of the Master, we remain comfortable.

He who thinks ill of the Perfect Satguru is killed by the Creator Himself.
This is the talk of the Court of the Lord. Nanak has realized this.

Now Guru Sahib says, "Whatever is happening in the court of the Lord, I am telling you that. And this is what is happening there: Those who think evil about the Masters are punished by God. Masters have no enmity, and if we criticize them, or oppose them, it is not good. Masters always pray for the welfare of the people and of all creatures. So if we have enmity with such great personalities, then definitely it is not just, and God always punishes."

Those who remember God while sleeping sing His praises when they wake up.
Such disciples are rare in the world who become one with the True Gurumukh.

There are a few who are connected with God, even while they are asleep, as well as when they are awake. Kabir Sahib says, "Whether I am sleeping or awake, I am always at the same place." Further, Kabir says, "I don't close my eyes, I don't plug my ears, I don't suffer any pain in my body, because I am seeing the beautiful form of my Master with my open eyes, and with all the happiness in my heart."

I sacrifice myself on those who speak the truth both day and night.

Now He says, "I sacrifice myself on those who are always connected with the meditation of Shabd Naam." Further, He requests the Lord: "O Lord, make us have the darshan of such people so that we may also come to you and we may also remain connected to the Shabd Naam."

God is responsible for everything – the point emphasized here – but it is *at the same time* true that He loves us and actively wants to bring us back to Him – all of us – and that we are responsible for the things which prevent us. See *The Jap Ji* (particularly p. 89, including the footnote) and *The Ocean of Love;* both books deal with this paradox very extensively.

Those who love the True One in body and mind go to the True Home.

Those who do the devotion of the Lord mentally, as well as physically—which means those who stay in meditation day and night—such people are welcome and are given a special place in the court of the Lord, the home of God; they are always honored. If we do the devotion of the Lord and if we search for God with our true heart, then definitely we become successful and we realize him.

Nanak utters the True Name and always worships the True One.

So in this little hymn, Guru Ramdas Ji has lovingly explained to us about the Shabd Naam and the importance of getting ourselves connected with It. He has told us about egoism, and how we are all suffering from this sweet disease. Mahatmas ask us: What things are we proud of? Are we proud of good health? Have we not seen any sick person—how his face becomes pale and how he feels so much weakness? So what is the use of having pride of good health, since it is a temporary thing? In the same way, why are we proud of our wealth? Have we not seen any poor person begging in the streets? Are we proud of our name and fame? Have we not seen people falling down and losing their name and fame? None of these things are worth being proud of because we can lose any of them at any time.

What is sleeping? What is waking?
Those who are Gurumukhs are acceptable.
He who remembers the Lord with every breath and morsel is the most perfect and excellent man.
By destiny one gets the Satguru, and the meditation is done day after day.
Those who remain in their company get honor in the court of the Lord.
Those who remember the Lord while sleeping also remember Him when they wake up.
Nanak says, Their faces are bright who when rising from sleep continually remember Him.
If we serve our Satguru we get limitless Naam.
He rescues those who are drowning in the ocean of life by giving them the gift of the Lord.
Blessed, blessed is that wholesale merchant who deals in the Naam.
The disciples - the retailers who come - are ferried across by means of the Shabd.
Nanak says, On whom grace is showered they serve the Creator.
Those men of the True One are the devotees of the Lord who meditate upon the True One.

Those Gurumukhs who have searched for and found the Path have realized the Truth within.
Those who serve the True Lord subdue and conquer the Negative Power.
The Perfectly True One is greater than all; and those who serve the True One are united with Him.
Praise to the Perfectly True One - by serving the True One one gets all the fruits.
The manmukh is a foolish creature.
Without Naam he is deluded.
Without the Master the mind does not become fixed.
Again and again he falls into the womb.
One meets the Satguru only if the Lord is gracious on him.
Nanak says, Praise the Naam so that the pain of birth and death might go.
I will praise my Guru with affection in many ways.
My mind is attuned to the Satguru. He himself has made this.
My tongue is not satisfied by praising Him so much.
My heart is turned towards the Lord.
Nanak has the hunger of Naam in His heart.

Having drunk the nectar of the Lord he becomes satiated.
The Perfectly True One is the Known Power who has made the day and night.
He is True who is always praising Him.
The greatness of the True One is True.
One who is praising Him is True and his praise is also true.
But no one has realized the value of the True One.
When one meets the Perfect Satguru then the Lord becomes present and comes into sight.
He who praises the True Gurumukh, all his hungers are ended.

11

The Condition of the Gurumukh

What is sleeping? What is waking?
Those who are Gurumukhs are acceptable.
He who remembers the Lord with every breath and morsel is the most perfect and excellent man.

Whenever God showers His grace and has mercy on humanity, He comes in the human body, because only a human being can teach a human being. Kabir Sahib says that Brahma speaks through the body of a human. How can even Brahma speak, without a body?

One kind of Saints, or the human beings in which God comes, are those who come from the Eternal Home and are Saints from the very beginning; and the other kind are those who get the Knowledge from the Saints who have come from the Eternal Home, and with their effort, reach the Eternal Home and make their soul free—they also become Saints. As one lamp is lit by another lamp and there is no difference between the light, in the same way, there is no difference between the Saints who come from the Eternal Home and the Saints who are prepared here.

Ever since our mind and soul have forgotten their Home they are wandering here and there outside. They have understood the material of the world as the ultimate truth and, becoming extroverted, they are wandering here and there in the worldly materials. Our mind has not thought about going back to its home, which is Brahm, nor has our soul had any thought about returning back to its Home, Sach Khand. It is not difficult to get a kingdom or power in this world, as compared to the difficulty of progressing spiritually. Both our mind and soul have the habit of wandering outside and they have become extroverted from ages and ages, and we have to gradually invert the attention of our mind and soul and make them introvert.

If we bring an uncivilized or wild man into our home where there are many modern comforts and good foods, because that man has the habit of remaining and living free in the forest, first of all he would not like to come with us into the house, but if we bring him there, he would not like to remain. He will feel very nervous and uncomfortable there, even though there are many things that can give him comfort. In the beginning, though, he won't appreciate them. He will be so nervous and upset that, if we don't stop him, he will try to run away and even start throwing things out of the house. But gradually, as he sits there in the house, and looks at the things which are present there, he starts getting interested in them. And as he begins to eat good foods and enjoy the comforts, he likes them so much that if we tell him to come out, he will not want to. Even if we force him to come out, he will not want to. In the beginning it was difficult to get him to remain in the house, but now that he knows how to enjoy the things which are there, it has become difficult to get him to come out.

Our mind also is in the same condition. Now it is very difficult for us to take our mind inside. And even if for once we take our mind inside, he doesn't necessarily want to stay. But if we become introverted and show our mind how many beauties there are lying within, and gradually develop the habit for our mind of enjoying those beauties, and when our mind starts tasting the nectar of Naam, then he starts getting interested in going within. The nectar of Naam is so sweet that once our mind has had the taste of It, he will never want to give that up. So, when we have forced our mind to go within, and after we have developed the habit of going within, then it becomes very difficult for us to come outside. Then our mind will always want to sit for meditation. Now, it is very difficult for us to take our mind within, as it is difficult to take that wild man within; but when our mind has visited the inner planes, when we have gone in the inner planes and enjoyed all the things there, then we will not want to waste a single minute. Whenever we get any time we will want to sit for meditation.

In this hymn Guru Sahib will describe the condition of the *Gurumukhs*—their importance, their qualities, how they are connected with the Lord, and how much love they have for the Masters. Gurumukhs are connected with the Lord all the time, whether they are asleep or awake. When they breathe in they are connected with the Lord, and when they breathe out, then also they are connected with the Lord. And they are always in love with the Lord.

Only such Gurumukhs are accepted in the Court of the Lord. And when Gurumukhs do anything—because Master is within them, God is within them—they are successful in whatever they do. And what is it that they do? Their works are to give us the Satsang, to meditate, and to make us meditate.

Guru Sahib says, "They always remain awake and they never sleep." When we, the worldly people, sleep, with our body our soul also sleeps. At that time our soul comes down from the eye center and spreads all over in the lower *chakras* or parts of our body, and whatever thoughts we have had during the day we are troubled by those thoughts and we have dreams according to them. Even in sleep, we are not at rest. As we were bothered by thoughts in the daytime, in the nighttime also we are bothered in the form of dreams. The thoughts change their form and they come down into the dreams and bother us. But when the Gurumukhs sleep, their soul doesn't come down into the lower chakras; their soul goes up into the higher planes. While their body is sleeping they are doing Satsang; they are giving inner Satsang to someone, or they are taking care of some souls. Whenever Masters sleep it is only their body which sleeps but their soul is still working.

Gurumukhs are so competent in their work of spirituality that if they are doing Satsang at one place physically, at the same time at many other places they appear and take care of the souls of the disciples. They give darshan to the disciple at some other place at the same time when they are doing Satsang physically at one place. And they are so very competent that, if they are traveling in this part of the world, right at that time they might be giving darshan and Satsang to other dear ones in other parts of the world. And yet they are very humble and always give the credit to their Master. Whenever dear ones have such experiences, they go to the Master and tell him, "Satguru, you gave us darshan at this time." At that time they don't become proud of that and they don't accept any credit for their own selves; they always say, "It is all the grace of Baba Ji."

Once in the satsang of Master Sawan Singh one young girl stood up and thanked Master for taking care of her grandmother's soul. She said, "I thank You, Master, very much because when my grandmother died You came and took her soul up." Master Sawan Singh said, "Thousands of grandmothers are dying, and always Baba Ji is coming and taking them up. It is not a new thing." At that time, Mastana Ji of Baluchistan was present there. He had brought some bones and ashes from some dead bodies whose souls had been received by Baba Sawan Singh Ji. So when Baba Sawan Singh said to that girl that thousands of grandmothers are dying and always Baba Ji (Baba Jaimal Singh, His Master) was coming, Mastana Ji stood up and said, "That is not true. You Yourself come to receive the souls of these dear ones." (Many people had died in that area, because of a cholera epidemic.) In India it is a tradition that when anybody dies they take some ashes or leftover bones which are not burnt, and they immerse them in the holy waters of the River Ganga or Jamna. So, Mastana Ji had brought the bones and ashes of those people, but instead of immersing them in the River Ganga or Jamna, he had brought them to Master Sawan Singh—because he used to say that Master Sawan Singh is the most holy place of pilgrimage.

By destiny one gets the Satguru, and the meditation is done day after day.
Those who remain in their company get honor in the court of the Lord.

We get those Satgurus Who are One with God only if we have very good karma. When God showers grace on us and when we have good karma, only then God brings us in the company of the Master. Often I have said in satsang, that the Perfect Masters who have done their meditation never criticize anyone and don't allow their disciples to criticize anyone. Guru Nanak Sahib says that the place where only one Naam is talked about is called satsang. The Naam is the Will of God which we can understand only by the grace of the Master. Guru Nanak says that that place where criticism and backbiting and other things are going on, cannot be called a place of satsang. Only that place is satsang where the people sing the praise and glory of Almighty Lord and the Master. Further he says, "Oh dear ones, you came in the company of the True One and found the sangat, and by coming in the sangat you will enjoy the true Nectar."

Those who remember the Lord while sleeping also remember Him when they wake up.
Nanak says, Their faces are bright who when rising from sleep continually remember Him.

Now he says that such Beloveds of God, whether they are asleep or awake, always remain connected with the Lord. When they get up they thank the Lord, and when they go to bed, then also they thank the Lord. He says that such Beloveds of God who thank Him day and night, get much honor in the Court of the Lord, and when they reach there, their faces are brightened and they are glorified. Such Beloveds of God feel that whatever breath they have taken without the remembrance of Master is illegal. They always understand any moments, any breaths, as useless and illegal in which they have not done the remembrance of Master. Guru Sahib says, "Oh Lord, if I forget You even for a moment, I will find a gap of fifty years."

If we serve our Satguru we get limitless Naam.
He rescues those who are drowning in the ocean of life by giving them the gift of the Lord.

First of all you should remember that our first job is to obey the commandments of the Master. If we obey, it becomes very easy to cross this ocean of life. Master Himself makes us sit in His boat of Naam and takes us across this ocean of life to our Home easily and safely.

Blessed, blessed is that wholesale merchant who deals in the Naam.
The disciples—the retailers who come—are ferried across by means of the Shabd.

Blessed is the Master Who came into this world as the True Merchant of Naam, and blessed are the disciples who went to Him and dealt in the merchandise of Naam. When the disciple comes to the Master, what is his work? What is the business in which the Master makes the disciple involved? That is the merchandise of Shabd Naam. Kabir Sahib says, "Oh Kabir, call him the poor one who doesn't have the wealth of Naam in his heart!"

Nanak says, On whom grace is showered they serve the Creator.
Those men of the True One are the devotees of the Lord who meditate upon the True One.
Those Gurumukhs who have searched for and found the Path have realized the Truth within.
Those who serve the True Lord subdue and conquer the Negative Power.
The Perfectly True One is greater than all; and those who serve the True One are united with Him.
Praise to the Perfectly True One— by serving the True One one gets all the fruits.

Truth is God, Which never gets destroyed, Which never goes away, and Which is permanent. Gurumukhs themselves are connected with that Ultimate Truth and They connect Their dear ones, Their disciples, also with that Truth. All the religious leaders are searching for God, but up until now no one has achieved peace, no one has realized God, by performing outer deeds and remaining in the outer religions. And in the future also that will never happen. Gurumukhs say that Shabd Dhun, or the Sound Current, is the Path, and Master is the One Who leads us on the Path.

The manmukh is a foolish creature.
Without Naam he is deluded.
Without the Master the mind does not become fixed.
Again and again he falls into the womb.

Now, after talking of the glory of God and telling us the qualities of the Gurumukh, now he is coming to the *manmukh*. He says that manmukhs are ignorant; they don't have any real knowledge because they are not introverted. They are doing the outer things; and unless they go within they cannot have the Knowledge of God. No matter how much hatha yoga we practice and try to control the mind in that way, we cannot do it. Instead of our mind coming under our control and being disciplined, it goes out of our control. Controlling the mind by hatha yoga and similar practices is just like putting on ashes to stop a fire; the fire is not stopped by that, it still goes on burning underneath, and when a strong wind blows the ashes away, again the fire starts burning in its full force. In the same way, if we are doing any other practices to control our mind, if we keep our mind disciplined, we may get a little bit of success and gain a little bit of control over the mind, but when the strong wind of the desires blows, those ashes or whatever discipline we have over the mind all goes away, and again the mind goes out of our control. Controlling the mind by practicing hatha yoga is just like controlling a snake by putting it in a box. We cannot remove its poison. He will have the same anger and hatred towards us, and whenever he gets a chance, whenever we open the box, he will at once bite us.

If we want to control the mind, first of all we need to know what our mind likes. And what is that thing by which we can control the mind? Masters tell us that mind is fond of pleasures of many different tastes. The most pleasure-giving thing is the Nectar of Naam, the Sound Current. You make him listen to the Sound Current and taste the elixir of Naam, and in that way your mind will come under your control.

He says, "Why are you thinking so much? Just kill your mind with the Naam of the Lord."

One meets the Satguru only if the Lord is gracious on him.

Nanak says, Praise the Naam so that the pain of birth and death might go.

Mahatmas whose eyes are opened, awakened Mahatmas, tell us that we can come in the company of the Masters only if we have the special grace and blessing of God. And when we come in the company of the Master and Master is merciful on us, only then can we take our soul back to the place from where it was separated.

History tells how the parents and the relatives of Guru Nanak were against Him. Out of His whole family only His sister and His brother-in-law recognized Him as the Master. Until God showers grace on us, we can never recognize the Master. Even if He comes to us by Himself, or if He starts living in our neighborhood, or even if He is born in our own house, still, unless God showers grace on us, we cannot recognize Him. The unfortunate ones never get the Master even if they sit with Him all the time.

I will praise my Guru with affection in many ways.
My mind is attuned to the Satguru. He himself has made this.

If you want to criticize, criticize your mind, because mind is the only thing which stands between us and the Master. And if you want to praise anyone, sing the praise and glory of the Master. If we make our mind sing the glory of the Master, our mind starts enjoying His company and tries to go within.

Kabir Sahib says that in all the three worlds and the nine divisions of this world, there is no one greater than Master. Master can do many things which even God cannot do. Saints and Mahatmas do not come as equals of God; they come as the Beloved Children of God, and they have bound their father in the chains of love. You know that the dear son can make his father do anything he wants. In the same way, Masters can make God do anything they want.

My tongue is not satisfied by praising Him so much.
My heart is turned towards the Lord.
Nanak has the hunger of Naam in His heart.
Having drunk the nectar of the Lord he becomes satiated.

The tongues of the true disciples never get tired or bored of singing the glory of their Master. Instead, they find it very delicious. They get great pleasure from singing the praise of their Master, and they remain contented as a blossomed flower when they see their Master. These are not the false lovers, they are the real lovers.

Mahatma Chatardas says, "The work which love can do, not even the sword can do that. The wound of love is so deep that it cannot be healed quickly, and only Love can heal the wound of love. The wound of the sword can be healed by medicine, but the wound of love cannot be healed unless the lover gets to see the Beloved. Our soul is a little one, but the love is so much that it becomes very difficult for the soul to bear it. And the condition of the lover is that he never has any attachment, he never likes to sleep, he never likes to eat a lot, he always remains in the remembrance of his Master. There is no other medicine for such a lover except the darshan of the Beloved."

The Perfectly True One is the Known Power who has made the day and night.
He is True who is always praising Him.
The greatness of the True One is True.
One who is praising Him is True and his praise is also True.
But no one has realized the value of the True One.
When one meets the Perfect Satguru then the Lord becomes present and comes into sight.
He who praises the True Gurumukh, all his hungers are ended.

Those who don't believe in the existence of God, and who say that there is no need to abstain from anything or to stop doing bad deeds because no one is going to ask for an account after we leave this world, who say that God is nowhere—they should think about this very patiently and with a cool heart. They should try to figure out what the Power is which is working behind the seen and unseen world. They should try to think, Who is taking care of this Creation? If they look at just a few things—if they only give their attention to the sunrise and the sunset—they should think about this: Who is the one who is making the sun rise at the exact time? And Who makes night come at the exact time? And Who is taking care of this Creation?

Gurumukhs come and tell us that whatever is happening in this world, God is working behind all these things, God Himself is doing them. They tell us that God doesn't reside anywhere outside; He is residing within each one of us. He is taking care of the Creation, and He is taking care of us also.

But how can we realize God? Gurumukhs tell us that God is within you. Therefore, you can realize Him only if you know how to go within.

Those who search for God with purity and truth in their heart, always get God because God is waiting for a man to become a noble man.

In the olden days when there were not many means of communication and it was not possible to spread the wisdom of the people everywhere, in India in those days there used to be at least one wise person—so called "wise person"—for every ten or fifteen villages.

Once it so happened that an elephant went to one village, and the villagers had never seen an elephant. But the elephant passed in the nighttime, and the next morning, when they saw the footsteps of the elephant, they were surprised, because they had never seen such a big creature, and they were trying to figure out what it meant. So they called that "wise person"; and when he came there, first he laughed and then he started weeping. So people asked him why he was doing that, and he said, "Listen—because I know what this is. Some man has done this. He has put many footsteps together and made a big footstep. I laughed because I know this thing and I am telling you. I am weeping because I was thinking what will happen to you when I die?—because I am the only wise person here and who will tell you all these good things? So that is why I wept."

Again it so happened that some people from another country brought one oil mill, which was run by bullocks. It had a big wooden shaft which they could attach to an animal, and when the animal moved, whether it was a horse or bullock or whatever, then that oil mill would move also. So when some people were carrying that oil mill in a bullock cart, the village people came and asked what it was. But they couldn't ask the people who were carrying it, so they all started speculating on it. When they couldn't reach any conclusion they called the same so-called "wise person," and he said, "Oh it is a very easy thing. It is that shaft of wood which God uses to put the soot in his eyes."*

The meaning of telling this is that when the wise people leave this world and only so-called "wise people" remain, then people start guessing about things; they start making up their own ideas. And whatever those so-called "wise people," who are not really wise, tell us, we believe. When few meditators remain in this world, and most meditators who have knowledge of God leave, people start forgetting the existence of God. They don't remember that God has not gone anywhere: God is within them. But because there is no one to tell them how to search for God, they start having their own ideas about God; and for guidance they go to people who have never seen God and who do not have any knowledge; and that is why, nowadays, many people do not believe in the existence of God, because there are only a few real meditators.

* In India, people use soot or lampblack for eye makeup applied with a rod or stick.

In the olden days, only those Mahatmas who had left their body and gone up into the inner planes, were preaching the Path of God – because they had practiced the Path of God. They wrote their experiences in the form of books for the guidance of the people; and only they were the preachers who had themselves practiced. But now there are paid preachers who don't have any meditation, who have not taken their soul up, who have not done any research in the Path of God; they are writing books. And by reading their experiences, we feel that we have done a lot of meditation, and we know a lot about God; and we don't bother to meditate. We read the book, and leave it aside, and fill ourselves up with pride and ego, thinking that we know a lot about the Path of the Masters; but we never put the words of the books into practice. When we get the information from reading the books, whether of the Masters or of other people, we should try to make those words part of our practical life, and only then can we rise above our Pind, our body, and get to Brahmand.

Kabir Sahib says, "O Brother, by reading the Vedas and other holy books one can never become worriless, and one can never realize God." Guru Nanak says, "O Nanak, even if you read millions of tons of books, still that will not do you any good. All the books which you have read will add to your ego, and you will not get to know the glory of Naam. Until you go within and become one with Naam, you cannot realize its glory."

Regarding those who read books day and night, and don't understand them, and don't put the words of the books into practice, Guru Nanak calls them, "the traders of the Vedas." Nanak says, "We will see when the traders of the Vedas take their souls up. Nobody can achieve any peace, and nobody can rise above, by reading books. We will see when these traders of books take their souls up." On the other hand, Guru Nanak says that the soul who meditates on the Naam of the Lord, whether he is learned or illiterate, he gets high status. If there is any best scripture or holy book, that is the human body; because all books are the creation of man. And if we search this human body, then we can get the knowledge of all books.

Masters don't mean to say that reading books is a bad thing. But They say that whatever we are reading, we should try to understand that. "Understanding" means that we have to give up the faults which we come to know after reading books; and after giving up the faults, we should try to do our meditation as written in the books.

If we act according to what is written in the books, if we go within, if we meditate, then our reading is worthwhile and useful, and we can have faith in the author who has written the book. So we should do the meditation of Shabd Naam and make our life successful.

Searching in my mind and body I found the Lord whom I was seeking;
I obtained the Master as the interceder who joined me with the Lord.
He who has assumed the Maya is blind and deaf.
He does not hear the Shabd and wanders about.
Those who meditate on Shabd by attuning themselves to it are called Gurumukhs.
They hear the Naam of the Lord, obey it, and become absorbed in it.
Whatever pleases Him He causes to happen.
Nanak says, The musical instrument sounds as it is made to sound.
You, O Creator, know everything that is going on within the creatures.
You, O Creator, are inestimable; the value of the whole world can be calculated.
Whatever exists is made by You. All is Your Creation.
You are present within every creature. Your work is true, O Lord.
Those who met the Satguru are united with the Lord.
They do not rely on anyone else.
This mind should be kept fast and the attention should be toward the Gurumukhs.
Why forget Him, with every breath and morsel, Who is within us while sitting or rising?

The worry about death and life goes away as
the soul is surrendered to the Lord.
Nanak says, As it pleases you, so keep me
and bestow the Naam.
The egoist manmukh does not know the
palace of the Lord.
One moment he is forward - one minute he is
backward.
He is always called to the palace but never
comes.
How can he get liberation in the court of
the Lord?
Some rare one knows the palace of the Satguru
and always remains with his hands folded.
Nanak says, On whom my Lord showers His
grace, He makes them return.
The performance of that seva is successful which
pleases the Satguru.
If Satguru is pleased, then all the sins run away.
The disciples hear with their ears the teachings
that are given by the Satguru.
Those who accept the Will of Satguru, they
prosper fourfold.
This way of the Gurumukhs is unique.
By seeing the Master and hearing Him their
minds are imbued with love.
He who conceals his own Guru does not get
any place or spot.

Both this world and that are lost, and he gets no place in the Court of the Lord.
That time does not come to hand that he may again go to the feet of the Satguru.
He is dropped from the account of the Satguru and he passes his life in pain.
The Satguru is a Supreme Being without enmity. Whom He wants, He attaches him to Himself.
Nanak says, The ones whom He has made to have the darshan are rescued in the Court of the Lord by Him.
The manmukh is ignorant, foolish and egotistical.
Within him is anger, and in gambling he has lost his intelligence.
He speaks falsely and earns the sins.
What does he hear and what does he speak?
He is blind and deaf. He goes astray and falls into a well.
The manmukh comes and goes blind.
Without meeting the Satguru he finds no place.
Nanak says, What was written before in his destiny, he earns that.
Whose hearts are hard toward the Lord do not sit near the Satguru.
There the Truth prevails - the hearts of the false ones are sad.

Practicing fraud and deceit they spend time.
Then they again go and sit with the false ones.
You see and ascertain it: falsehood does not mingle with Truth.
The false ones mingle with the false ones,
Whereas the truthful disciples sit with the Satguru.

12

In the Company of the Saints

Searching in my mind and body I found the Lord whom I was seeking;
I obtained the Master as the interceder who joined me with the Lord.

All secrets, all realities, and all facts which exist are within our human body. Whatever we see outside, God has created within also.

It is like the radio: people play music, play drums, dance, sing and do all sorts of things—and we listen to all this through the radio. If anyone thinks they can break the radio and take out the dancers, singers and musicians, that is not possible; because they are not physically there; only their voices are broadcast through there.

Our body is like a radio set, within which all the Khands and Brahmands (higher planes) and the entire creation, seen or unseen, is lying. Not in their physical form, of course; they are in their astral or causal form. And if anybody thinks that by operating on the body he can take out the Khands and Brahmands, that is not possible. Just as the radio will not work until it is connected with a battery or with power and tuned to a station, in the same way if our body is not connected with the "battery" and is not tuned properly, we cannot know about the inner world, the Khands and Brahmands.

Who connects our "battery" and what is it? Our battery is the Shabd, the Power of God. And the Masters who have manifested the Power in them, connect our "set," our soul, with that Power, that "battery." And when we are in tune, then we can easily get messages and things from the Brahmand.

So Guru Sahib says, "When I searched for God with all my mind and body, then I realized Him. But I saw that without the help of someone in-between, He could not be realized." He says, "When the yearning for realizing God came within me, I searched for Him everywhere, using my body and mind. And when I saw that we cannot realize Him unless we have Someone to intercede between us and God, then I felt the necessity of the Master." Master is like a lawyer who wins the suit for us, who helps us solve the problem of realizing God. In the world, if we want to win some lawsuit, we need a lawyer who can help us. Without him it is more than we can handle. In the same way, if we want to solve this question, this "suit," of realizing God, we need a lawyer, and he is the Master.

He who has assumed the Maya is blind and deaf.
He does not hear the Shabd and wanders about.
Those who meditate on Shabd by attuning themselves to it are called Gurumukhs.
They hear the Naam of the Lord, obey it, and become absorbed in it.

We are sleeping in a deep sleep, because we are intoxicated by Maya; and that is why we are not able to hear the Sound of the Lord, which is sounding within us day and night, even though God is sounding that Sound within us all the time. And moreover we are not able to have the darshan of the Light which God has kept within us, because we are intoxicated by Maya. We have become deaf and blind.

Whatever pleases Him He causes to happen.
Nanak says, The musical intrument sounds as it is made to sound.

God has kept everything in His hands. He decides whom He has to make a Gurumukh and whom He has still to send in the cycle of births and deaths. The condition of the jivas is like musical instruments: it is up to the player to play whichever way he wants to play. The instrument cannot do anything. In the same way, it is all up to God. Only He knows how He has to play us.

This doesn't mean that we should stop working. When we know that God makes us do everything and that it is all in the hands of God, it doesn't mean that we should stop working at whatever we are supposed to do. We should always try our best, use our intellect, and go on working.

Once Prophet Mohammed was telling his disciples that everything is in the Will of God; God Himself does everything. So at that time one of his lazy disciples got up (one who used to guard the camels at night), and said, "Then, Master, that means that now I don't need to take care of the camels. I don't need to tie them, I don't need to stay up and watch them, because you say that God does everything. The thieves are even sent by God, and everything happens in the Will of God, so what is the use of staying up and giving pain to the body?" Prophet Mohammed said, "No. No doubt, everything happens in the Will of God and God Himself is the Doer. But the work which *you* are given to do, the work which you are supposed to do, you should do that. You should tie the camels, you should stay up and guard the camels. And if after you do all this work, if *still* in the Will of God the thieves come and take the camels away, it means that God didn't want the camels to be with us." So whatever work we are given, whatever things we are supposed to do, we should do that wholeheartedly. But we should always leave the results for God to decide, because everything happens in the Will of God.

You, O Creator, know everything that is going on within the creatures.
You, O Creator, are inestimable; the value of the whole world can be calculated.

Now Guru Sahib says, "O Lord, You know everyone. You know who is good, who is bad, to whom You have to give darshan, and to whom You don't have to give the darshan. And no one can delude You by his cleverness."

You know about all the creatures whom You created—You know the number of them—because after giving them birth, You didn't forget them. That is why You always bring birth and death at the destined time. You have never forgotten how many creatures You have created; You always remember them. But the poor souls cannot remember. They do not know when You came into existence, because the poor souls are in Your hands, and they don't know anything about You.

Whatever exists is made by You. All is Your Creation.
You are present within every creature. Your work is true, O Lord.
Those who met the Satguru are united with the Lord.
They do not rely on anyone else.

Now he lovingly says, "O Lord, in a unique way and very beautifully, You are residing in everyone, You are present in every heart. But how do we know this? We can know this secret, we can get convinced of this fact, only when we go in the company of the Gurumukhs and when the Gurumukhs give us Naam and make us realize You. Only then do we become convinced that You reside everywhere. Once we have seen You in our own selves, we see You working everywhere in everybody's heart. And after that, we don't need to come back into this suffering world again."

> **This mind should be kept fast and the attention should be toward the Gurumukhs.**
> **Why forget Him, with every breath and morsel, Who is within us while sitting or rising?**

If we want to meet God, if we have a real yearning for God, first of all we need a pure mind. And then we need determination. We should be determined to meet God, we should always give preference to this work of realizing God; only after that we should take care of the world. That is why he says that the Simran which our Satgurus have given to us, we should do that day and night, whether we are sitting, standing, asleep or awake. All the time we should do the Simran of the Masters.

But what is our condition? Our heart is weak and we are not strong in our determination, but we try to imitate the lovers of God. We try to realize God by talking, but as far as walking in the Path of Love is concerned, we walk backwards.

> **The worry about death and life goes away as the soul is surrendered to the Lord.**
> **Nanak says, As it pleases you, so keep me and bestow the Naam.**

When we practice the teachings of the Gurumukhs, we control our mind. And when we have control of our mind, it makes no difference if we are criticized or we are praised, if pain comes or happiness comes. Because when we have controlled our mind—when we have practiced the teachings of the Masters—whatever we get, we understand all that as coming in the Will of God. If we are criticized, we understand it as the Will of God; if we are praised, then also we give credit to the Lord; if pain comes, we accept that in the Will of God; and if we get happiness, we become grateful to the Will of God.

> **The egoist manmukh does not know the palace of the Lord.**

One moment he is forward—one minute he is backward.
He is always called to the palace but never comes.
How can he get liberation in the court of the Lord?

Those who obey their mind get caught up in ego, and when Masters call them, when Masters tell them, "Come on, come in, come within, go up, go to the inner planes, go to your Real Home," at that time they don't pay any attention to the words of Master; they don't take any advantage of the presence of Master. But when the Masters leave, then they repent.

Some rare one knows the palace of the Satguru and always remains with his hands folded.
Nanak says, On whom my Lord showers His grace, He makes them return.

There are very few people who know the home of the Lord. Those who do know the home of the Lord and go there have a lot of humility and meekness and are always very humble. They keep their hands folded before their Master, and they say, "Without You, we are nothing. Whatever we have, that all belongs to You, and whatever position we have got, that is all because of You." Only those who have that much humility within, can enter the home of the Lord.

Hazur Maharaj Ji used to say that if you want to meet God, first of all you should develop humility. Because God is Almighty—He has everything except humility. He doesn't have humility because He is All in All, He is Almighty. Before whom should He show humility?

The performance of that seva is successful which pleases the Satguru.
If Satguru is pleased, then all the sins run away.

Only that seva to the Master is accepted which we do according to the instructions of the Master. If Master tells us to cut the grass, and if we cut the grass according to His instructions, He is pleased and our seva is accepted. If Master tells us to do anything else, and we do it according to His instructions, only that seva is accepted. Those who do the seva of the Master according to the instructions of the Master, all their sins are removed and they become able to realize God.

Once a dear one whose name was Bhai Biddi Chand came to Guru Har Gobind, the sixth Guru of the Sikhs. Before coming to the Master he had been a thief, and when he applied for Initiation the Master told him that he could get Initiation only if he promised that he would stop doing his work and not rob anymore. So he said, "Okay, I will not do this work," and he got Initiation. So when he got Initiation, you know that habit is after all, habit: it is very difficult to change habits. So even though he was given Initiation and he started coming to satsang, still, sitting in the satsang he would think about stealing things and harassing people. He started going to the place in the satsang where people left their shoes, but when he tried to steal some shoes he at once remembered that his Master had told him not to do this job any more and that he had promised that he would not when he applied for Initiation. So he thought, "Well, Master has told me not to take these away but at least I can change their places." So he took the shoes from one side and he put them on the other side so that people would think that somebody had stolen them. The people were bothered a lot, and they complained to the Master. When they confronted Bhai Biddi Chand he said, "Listen, Master told me not to steal them. But he didn't tell me that I couldn't change their places. So I am obeying the orders of the Master—I am not stealing them!"

Our condition is like that. When Master tells us not to do one thing, we obey that particular word. But we change the form of His order, and we don't apply it very deeply. We may give up doing that act outwardly, but within, we keep doing that act. Master tells us not to hate people. We may abide by that outwardly, but within we have hatred. That is why we never progress.

The disciples hear with their ears the teachings that are given by the Satguru.
Those who accept the Will of Satguru, they prosper fourfold.

Masters tell us how we have to listen to the Sound, and how we have to meditate. So those who obey the instructions of the Master—those who abstain from the things they are told to abstain from—and those who listen to the Sound Current according to the instructions of the Master, they know how to remain happy in the Will of God. And those who remain happy in the Will of God—those who accept the Will of God in all circumstances—Master blesses them in abundance. Master Sawan Singh Ji used to say that when the potter makes the pot, from the outside he may hit the pot, but from the inside he holds his hand so that the pot doesn't break. In the same way, when Master is giving us a blessing—when Master is putting us to a test—from outside He may be very hard, but from inside He has kept His soft hand, so that we may not break down. If we know how to remain happy in the Will of God, we can get more blessings from Him.

> **This way of the Gurumukhs is unique.**
> **By seeing the Master and hearing Him their minds are imbued with love.**
> **He who conceals his own Guru does not get any place or spot.**
> **Both this world and that are lost, and he gets no place in the Court of the Lord.**

Those who hide their Masters get no honor in this world; in fact, they lose everything. God will never appreciate them.

> **That time does not come to hand that he may again go to the feet of the Satguru.**
> **He is dropped from the account of the Satguru and he passes his life in pain.**

First of all, people obey their mind and go away from their Master. But whenever they get trapped in any problem, or when they get sick, they remember Master, and when they are helped, then they repent that they left the Master earlier. You know that many people when they get some problem or when they realize their mistakes, they come back to the Path of the Masters.

The seed of Naam which is sown by the Master within anyone will definitely sprout and grow. There is no power in this world which can destroy that seed.

> **The Satguru is a Supreme Being without enmity. Whom He wants, He attaches him to Himself.**
> **Nanak says, The ones whom He has made to have the darshan are rescued in the Court of the Lord by Him.**

Masters are without enmity; they have no enemies, because God has showered a lot of grace on them and has given them a lot of love. They see God working everywhere, and they are very gracious: whoever has their darshan gets liberated in the Court of the Lord. The Negative Power doesn't accept such souls who have had the darshan of the Master.

Master Sawan Singh Ji used to tell the story very often about a merchant who went to a village to reclaim the loan which he had given to a farmer. That farmer was very poor and he had nothing to give to him. So the merchant took all his belongings and made the farmer homeless. The farmer was so upset that he told him that he would not help him in taking his things to the nearby town from where that merchant had come. Looking at his condition, the other farmers also thought that there was no need to help that man, because he was very cruel. "Today he has mistreated our brother, tomorrow he can do the same thing with us, so we should boycott him and not help him."

That merchant needed someone to take his luggage to the town, so he was looking for someone but no one came up to help him. There was one mahatma there who was seeing all this, and he felt very gracious on that merchant and said, "I will help you in taking the luggage to the town, but there is a condition: either you tell a story to me and I will nod – I will say, yes, yes – or I will tell you a story and you should listen to it, very carefully."

That merchant thought there could not be any cheaper bargain than this, so he said, "Okay, Mahatma Ji, you carry the luggage and tell me a story, and I will listen to it, and pay attention to it."

The Mahatma was very gracious – Masters are always very gracious. They tell us stories; the meaning of their telling stories to us is not that they want to entertain us – they tell us a story so that we may listen to the story and see what faults we have. That Mahatma told him many stories, and through his stories he told him what faults he had. So gradually, as he was going on telling him stories, that merchant realized his faults.

When they came near the town that Mahatma told him, "Okay, now take your luggage and go. But let me tell you one thing: You have realized that in your whole life you haven't done a single good thing, you have no good karma, and you will not get any fruit of good karma. You have done only one good deed – you have spent this hour with me. And you will get the benefit of it. When you go to the Lord of Judgment they will ask you if you want to enjoy the fruit of this good karma before going to hell, or if you want to do it later. You should tell them that you want to come to me before going to hell, and when you come to me then you will realize how very important it was for you to be in my company. Because this is the only good deed which you have done."

When that merchant died he went to the Lord of Judgment, and the Lord of Judgment looked at his account and told him, "Well, you don't have any good karma in your account except for one thing: you spent one hour with a mahatma. Because of that you will be allowed to go and see him once again, but only for a few moments. Do you want to do that before going to hell, or do you want to save that until later?"

The merchant remembered what the Mahatma had told him, so he said, "Who knows when I will come out of hell? Let me go to see that Mahatma and express my gratitude to him, before going to hell." So the Lord of Judgment sent the angels of death with him and told him that he could go to the plane where the Mahatma was living; and since the angels of death were not allowed to go there, he should go there alone, and after two moments when the angels of death tell him by signs that his time is up, he should come back.

So when that merchant came to the Mahatma, Mahatma said, "Dear one, so you have come." He said, "Yes, Mahatma, I have come, but I'm afraid that I will have to leave very soon because the angels of death are waiting for me. They have told me to come back after two moments. So what should I do? I am very afraid." So the Mahatma said, "Don't worry. Keep quiet. Sit down here. Don't worry about them, don't pay any attention to them, because they cannot enter this place."

Then that merchant realized how very important it was for him to be in the company of the Master. Because, when he came in the company of the Master, he was allowed to see Him once again for two moments; but because that Mahatma was very gracious and loving towards him, He forgave him all his sins and paid off all his karmas, and liberated him from all the sufferings of hell.

So when the Masters give us their loving, gracious darshan, at that time they are showering a lot of grace on us. The company of the Master is always valuable. We people don't realize how much we are getting by coming in the company of the Masters, but we will realize it when we go in the court of the Lord.

The manmukh is ignorant, foolish and egotistical.
Within him is anger, and in gambling he has lost his intelligence.

Now he tells us about the manmukhs. The manmukh has qualities of anger, hatred, egoism, jealousy, greed, and all the bad qualities which mind can create, and when he is swayed by the wave of anger, he loses all his wisdom, and feels like that gambler who loses everything.

He speaks falsely and earns the sins.
What does he hear and what does he speak?

Obeying their mind, such people always lie. What knowledge can such a person give people? What can people get from him?

He is blind and deaf. He goes astray and falls into a well.
The manmukh comes and goes blind.
Without meeting the Satguru he finds no place.
Nanak says, What was written before in his destiny, he earns that.
Whose hearts are hard toward the Lord do not sit near the Satguru.
There the Truth prevails—the hearts of the false ones are sad.

Those whose hearts are hard, who don't have any love and affection for God, even if they come in the Satsang of the Master, they cannot take advantage of it, because when the Master speaks the Truth, they cannot accept it; they have no softness in their hearts and they don't like it.

Practicing fraud and deceit they spend time. Then they again go and sit with the false ones.
You see and ascertain it: falsehood does not mingle with Truth.

Such souls, even if they come in the presence of the Master, spend their time in tricks. Sometimes, they will look at the ground, sometimes somewhere else; they cannot look at the Master, because they are not true to their own Selves. When the meeting is over, they go and join the critic, and do the same work.

You may try your best but you cannot manifest lies or false things in the true souls. When true souls come into the Satsang, no matter how much other people, the critics, tell them, "you should not go there, you should not do this and you should not do that"; for those souls it has no effect. They do not take such advice, and they keep coming to the Satsang.

The false ones mingle with the false ones,
Whereas the truthful disciples sit with the Satguru.

Those who are the false ones, those who are dealing in refuse, and those who are criticizing, all join together at one place. Whereas the true souls, those who are doing the meditation of Shabd Naam, go in the presence of the Master and do the meditation of Shabd Naam, and they make their lives successful.

He Himself, making efforts, destroyed the remaining critics.
Nanak says, Those who help the Saints are present everywhere.
Those who have forgotten from the very beginning, where can they put their hands?
Nanak says, They are destroyed by the Almighty Doer.
Taking nooses they go in the night, but the Lord knows all His creatures.
They look at another's wife, hiding themselves away.
They break holes in the walls of houses in a rough place and enjoy sweet liquor.
They themselves will repent of their own deeds.
The Angel of Death will press them like sesame seeds in an oil mill.
Only the servants of the True Emperor are accepted.
Nanak says, Those who serve others are ignorant and die in pain.
The destiny which is written by the Lord cannot be erased.
Nanak says, Meditate on the Naam of the Lord - which is the wealth and capital.
To whom the Lord has put a stumbling block, where will he put his foot?
He always tastes poison who is committing

countless sins. He dies in pain, criticizing.
In his body he burns.
Who can protect him who is destroyed by the True Lord?
Nanak says, I am in the refuge of the Alakh Being.
There are many pains in the deep hells- which are the places for the ungrateful one.
Nanak says, Those who do not become grateful are destroyed by the Lord.
There are remedies for all diseases, but there is no medicine for the critic.
Nanak says, He who has forgotten the Lord suffers a lot and goes in the womb again.
The Perfect Satguru gives the unending wealth of the Lord.
All worries are erased and the fear of Yama ceases.
Lust, anger, and bad qualities are destroyed in the company of the Sadhus.
Those who serve other than the True One will die becoming crippled.
Nanak says, Master has blessed the Naam. Remain attached to it.

13

The Highest Window

He Himself, making efforts, destroyed the remaining critics.
Nanak says, "Those who help the Saints are present everywhere."

Guru Ramdas Ji Maharaj has told us the story of the *tapa,* that yogi who opposed Guru Amardas, and he has told us the condition of the manmukhs—those who obey their mind—and he told us the condition of those who take Inititiation from the Master and turn away from Him, and of those who criticize the Perfect Master. Further, he has told us the qualities of the Gurumukhs, and he told us how to differentiate between the Gurumukhs and the manmukhs. He has told us about those who obey their mind, how their mind drags them to hell and how they are not able to do the meditation of Shabd Naam. And he has told us many other things regarding the Path of the Masters in a very beautiful way.

Now the same bani is continued and on the same subject, but now the fifth Guru, Guru Arjan Dev Ji Maharaj, True Lord, is continuing this bani and He will comment on the same subject.

Guru Arjan Dev was a very peaceful Mahatma—He was very quiet-natured and He had done a lot of meditation. The love which He had for his Master is very obvious by reading this bani. His bani will tell us very clearly how much love He had for his Master. He says, "When I had good fortune—when God showered grace on me—He made me realize Himself within me, with the grace and help of my Master. And that is why I sacrifice myself on my Master, Guru Ramdas Ji, because He made me see God within myself."

Once Guru Arjan Dev was sent to Lahore from Amritsar. Guru Ramdas Ji used to live in Amritsar and He sent Guru Arjan Dev to

Lahore. Lahore and Amritsar are not very far away from each other; it's a difference of only a few miles. But Guru Arjan Dev was having so much pain of separation from his Master, that he said, "If I don't see You even for a moment, I feel that the Kali Yuga—or the Negative Age—has made its impression on me. Now, when am I going to see You? Oh Lord, tell me when I'm going to come back and when I'm going to see You. I cannot sleep at night—I spend the night counting the stars. And I don't like anything. Please, Oh Lord, shower grace on me, and call me back so that I may have Your darshan, because if I don't have Your darshan even for a moment, I feel that the Negative forces are making impressions on me." This is the type of love Guru Arjan Dev had for his Master.

Guru Ramdas left Guru Arjan Dev to guide the sangat, and apart from guiding the sangat, Guru Arjan Dev did a great work which is still helping the practitioners of the Path of the Masters. He worked very hard, collected the writings of all the Mahatmas who had done the meditation of Shabd Naam, and compiled those writings and edited them and formed them into the book which we call Guru Granth Sahib. The Guru Granth Sahib was compiled by Guru Arjan Dev Ji.

Guru Arjan Dev had an elder brother named Prithia. Prithia was very much against Guru Arjan Dev, because even though he was older than Guru Arjan Dev, still he was not appointed as the successor to his father. So he went to the Emperor Jahangir along with another dear one called Chandu Savai. They both told the Emperor that Guru Arjan had compiled a Granth, a book, in which there was criticism of the Muslim religion. Emperor Jahangir asked for the Guru Granth Sahib many times, but he couldn't do anything because whenever they read they didn't find even a single word of criticism. Because there is no criticism in the Guru Granth Sahib; all that is written in the Guru Granth Sahib is regarding the Shabd Naam and the Master.

Because of the opposition, Emperor Jahangir called for Guru Arjan Dev in Lahore and asked him for a lot of money, millions of rupees. And when Guru Arjan Dev said, "I don't have that much money in my home," because of the other people, Guru Arjan Dev was tortured to death by Emperor Jahangir. He was made to sit on hot coals while burning sand was poured on his head, and once he was made to stand in a big container of boiling water. In this way he was given a very hard time.

Even though he was tortured to death, still he never cursed anyone nor had any bad thoughts for anyone. When he was being tortured, Mian Mir, one of the dear ones, came there and when he saw that Guru Arjan Dev was sitting on the hot coals in the remembrance of Master, Mian Mir told Him, "Guru Dev, if you order me, I can raze the city of Lahore to the ground." But Guru Arjan Dev replied, "No, dear one. I could also do that. But that is not the Will of God. It is much better to be in the Will of God. I like the Will of God, it's very sweet. So you should not do that." He said, "O Lord, I like Your Will – It is very sweet. And Nanak always prays for the boon of Naam. Humility is my shield, and no one can stand in front of this shield."

If anyone criticizes the Master, or if anyone troubles the Master, the Masters do not imitate them – the Masters do not respond back with trouble and criticism. They do not lose their quality, They do not lose Their grace which God has given Them. They do not misuse the grace and the power which God has given Them, and They do not do anything against Their critics and those who give them a hard time. Instead of cursing and thinking ill of them, Masters always pray for their well-being. They request to God, "O Lord, please shower grace on them so that they may realize what they are doing." So that is why he says here that if anyone criticizes the Beloved of God, the Beloved of God doesn't lose His quality.

So far, all the successful Masters, prophets, rishis, munis, and all the great sages and seers who came in this world and were successful in their practices never criticized anyone. And they have told their disciples to abstain from criticism. Master Sawan Singh used to say that the critic always finds the means to become mean. He used to say that people get pleasure from indulging in other bad things, but they don't get anything from criticizing, because it is tasteless – it is neither sour nor sweet – but still, it is amazing, it is a pity, how people are attached to it, how day and night people indulge in criticism.

Everyone is carrying two bags: one in front and one in back. We always keep our bad qualities and faults in the bag on our back and we never count them or pay any attention to them. But we do not keep our front bag clean either because when we criticize others we take their faults and put them in our front bag. So that is why we are plundered; when we criticize others we take their bad qualities, and in that way we become worse and worse. Kabir Sahib said,"Looking at other people's faults, you are happy and you are enjoying and are pleased; but you never pay any attention to your own faults which have no limits."

Guru Arjan Dev Ji says here that those who criticize and trouble the Saints, God does punish them. He Himself hands over such souls to the Negative Power; and Negative Power gives them punishment. And because Beloveds of God are the dear Sons of God, God always protects Them and takes care of Them as a mother takes care of her children. So Masters are always under the protection of God, and no matter if They are criticized or tortured to death, still They always remain happy in the Will of God because They are in His protection.

Those who have forgotten from the very beginning, where can they put their hands?
Nanak says they are destroyed by the Almighty Doer.

Now Guru Arjan Dev Ji Maharaj says, "What can the poor souls do? There is nothing in their hands." Because those who are made by God to forget from the very beginning, how can they realize? How can they be aware? And those who are made by God to drown, from where can they ask for help? And how can they be saved?

Taking nooses they go in the night but the Lord knows all his creatures.
They look at another's wife, hiding themselves away.

God has created this earth and He Himself has created all the creatures on this earth. So as man has the right to live on this earth, in the same way other creatures, animals and insects, also have an equal right to share this earth and live on this earth. If we kill the animals for our food, and if someone tells us that we should not do that, we argue: we say, "Why has God created them, if we are not supposed to eat them?" Mahatmas have a very good answer for that. They say, "Just imagine, if someone kills you for his food, what will you feel? Will you feel pain or happiness?"

We know that when the doctor prepares an injection to put into our body even though he is doing a good thing for us, still we feel pain in this body of six feet. But have we ever thought of our future? If, because of our bad karmas, we get the body of an animal, and if those who are animals now get the human body and if they have a sword in their hand and our neck is under their sword, what will we feel? Will we feel pain, or happiness?

So here Guru Arjan Dev Ji Maharaj says, "Oh man, we are killing for our pleasure." All that is counted, and we will definitely get the punishment for it. Whether we are killing an animal, or bird, or anything like that, we will definitely get the punishment for it. God is looking at all our actions. And further he says that if we are enjoying with people to whom we are not married, now we may feel pleasure coming from that, but when we will go in the Court of the Lord we will be given punishment there. Master Sawan Singh Ji used to say that those men or women who indulge with other men and women, they might feel pleasure and happiness here, but when they will go they will go in hell, they will be made to embrace heated pillars. It is a grave sin. Guru Gobind Singh Ji says that God may hear the call of the man later, but He hears the call of the ant sooner. Don't think that when we are killing animals or doing other bad deeds there is no one who is keeping account and we will not get punishment for it. God is for everyone, God takes care, God nourishes and protects even the animals and the little creatures. And if we kill them, we definitely have to get punishment for that, because God is keeping all the accounts.

After creating this creation, God didn't become worriless, He didn't forget the world. Right after He created the Creation He started sending the rishis, munis, prophets, Masters and great Saints to set limits and make laws; to make people aware of the laws of Nature. And that is why, when the rishis, munis, great Masters and prophets come into this world, They tell us what is the good path and what is the bad path; They tell us how we are to give up our bad habits and turn to good habits. And They even tell us that human beings are superior to other creatures because God has blessed them with intelligence and sense. He can understand the sense of good and bad much more than the animals can. And because God has made us superior in all the Creation, we are expected to do certain things. So whatever we are doing that goes against the Law of Nature, we definitely have to get punishment for that. The government has made the law for criminals, and if anyone disobeys the law and murders someone and is caught and given punishment, if he repents and asks for forgiveness, he cannot be forgiven. He would be told that he should suffer this punishment, and next time he should not do that. When we go against the law, we definitely have to go to jail and get punished. In the same way when we go against the Law of Nature, then also we are punished.

Saints and Mahatmas have made the laws. The *banis,* or the writings of the Masters, are the laws. They tell us that God has given us eighty-four lakhs of births and deaths, and if we waste it without doing the devotion of the Lord, we will be punished. Masters tell us in their laws what are the good things for us to do and what are the bad things. They tell us, don't think that you will not get punished for those deeds which you are doing in secret and which you think that nobody else except you knows about it, so it is not a sin (you think). You know that when we do any good deed, any pious deed—such as giving—we try our best to show people how many good deeds we have done. But nobody consults anyone when he is committing any bad deed. But you know that in this world people are suffering the reactions of their bad deeds as well as enjoying the fruits of their good deeds, so we are getting punishment for the bad deeds which we are doing and not showing people. Masters tell us, "Don't think that the bad deeds you are hiding from people can be hidden from God; nothing can be hidden from God because God is within you, and He is aware of your every single action."

Kabir Sahib says, "Oh ignorant man! You have committed sins and you have hidden them, and you think that nobody will know about that. But they all will come out when you go to the Lord of Judgment." Mahatmas whose eyes are opened tell us that all that we are doing here is all being recorded like a videotape. The Lord of Judgment is not dependent on any witness. He will not ask anyone. He will not let us prove ourself worthy and good. He will play the videotape, the recording which he is making now, and we will have no excuse. Everything that we have done in this world will be very clear, and we ourselves will be able to see what we did.

Sitting in the highest window, the Lord is looking at all the deeds of the people, and whatever amount of His devotion they are doing, they are getting benefit.

They break holes in the walls of houses in a rough place and enjoy sweet liquor.
They themselves will repent of their own deeds.

God has no enemy—He is without enmity—He has only love for everyone. But whatever deeds people have done, they enjoy or suffer according to that. When we do deeds, when we develop karmas, at that time we don't realize that we will have to suffer or enjoy their reaction. We repent when we go into the next life, or in the same life later on when we have to suffer the reactions of our bad deeds. Then we realize and then we repent. But at that time we cannot do anything. Whatever karmas we have done we will have to suffer for them.

The Lord Who decides about our punishment—the Lord Who looks at our accounts, at our deeds, and decides which punishment we should be given—that God of Judgment gives the punishment to our astral body. The physical body doesn't get any punishment because it doesn't go there; but our astral body gets the punishment. And those who do many bad deeds, their body is made to pass through the mill, and they are churned, and they are given many other troubles.

The Angel of Death will press them like sesame seeds in an oil mill.
Only the servants of the True Emperor are accepted.
Nanak says, "Those who serve others are ignorant and die in pain."

Who are accepted by God? Only those who are meeting the Masters, doing the meditation, serving the Masters and obeying them—only they are accepted by God. And those who turn away from the Masters—those who don't do the devotion of the Master and don't serve the Master—those who practice other things other than the practices shown by the Master, they take birth, die, go from one body to another, and they are not accepted by God.

The destiny which is written by the Lord cannot be erased.
Nanak says, "Meditate on the Naam of the Lord—which is the wealth and capital."

Even before we were born—before we came in the womb of the mother—our destiny was written out; our fate, our pralabdha karma was written; and according to that we have to experience profits and losses. All that was predetermined. And that is why no matter how much we may try to avoid them still we get the results that we are supposed to have. These pralabdha karmas are determined by our past, and no one can increase or decrease them.

However, if we come in the company of the Master and remain in Their guidance, the Masters take on some of our karma Themselves; They pay it off in that way. But there are some karmas which we ourselves have to pay and which no one else can pay; the Masters advise us to pay off those karmas lovingly and happily in the Will of God.

To whom the Lord has put a stumbling block, where will he put his foot?
He always tastes poison who is committing countless sins; He dies in pain, criticizing. In his body he burns.
Who can protect him who is destroyed by the True Lord?
Nanak says, "I am in the refuge of the Alakh Being."

Those who are selected by God to do this negative work cannot come to Him and will not be able to do His devotion as long as they eat the poison of criticism. Day and night they go on criticizing and because of that they go on developing their karmas. Guru Arjan Dev Ji Maharaj says that the critics are not only burning from the outside—their body is burning within also.

He continues, "But we are very fortunate ones because our Master, Guru Ramdas Ji, showered a lot of grace on us and has made us see the Alakh God, Whom we cannot comprehend."

There are many pains in the deep hells—which are the places for the ungrateful one.

We know that in this world those who are good people are not troubled, but for criminals the jails and prisons are ready. In the same way, God has created hells and heavens and moreover He has created His Eternal Home—the Eternal Home of Souls, Sach Khand. We know that ideally nobody sends the good people into the jails; only criminals are sent to jail. So Guru Arjan Dev Ji Maharaj says that in hell there is a lot of suffering, and that place is made for those who don't do the devotion of the Lord.

Nanak says, "Those who do not become grateful are destroyed by the Lord."

Who gets beatings and sufferings in the hells? Only those who do not do the devotion of the Lord, who do not become grateful to the Lord. Before starting the meditation daily I have said that the devotion of the Lord is the precious wealth, and those who work hard to earn this wealth, they definitely become wealthy with the wealth of the devotion of the Lord. The devotion of the Lord is like nectar and it removes lust, anger, greed, attachment and egoism. Those who search for God and devote themselves to God with their whole heart and with true yearning, they always become successful.

There are remedies for all diseases but there is no medicine for the critic.
Nanak says, "He who has forgotten the Lord suffers a lot and goes in the womb again."

In this world people have made medicines for almost all diseases; they have made medicine for dysentery, diarrhea, constipation; for the problems of eyes, ears; for almost everything. But God has not made any medicine for the critics. Because God Himself makes the critic forget. Nanak says, "He goes in the cycle of birth and death." No matter where the critic goes, whether he becomes a learned man or not, no matter what he does, still he cannot be forgiven. Because when God doesn't want to forgive him, when God wants him to go in the cycle of birth and death, then who can shower grace on him?

The Perfect Satguru gives the unending wealth of the Lord.
All worries are erased and the fear of Yama ceases.

Lust, anger, and bad qualities are destroyed in the company of the Sadhus.
Those who serve other than the True One will die becoming crippled.
Nanak says, "Master has blessed the Naam. Remain attached to it."

Guru Sahib talks about the qualities of his Master and he glorifies Him. He says, Our Master Guru Ramdas was very gracious on us and that is why we came in His company—because God was gracious on us. And when we came in the company of the Master He taught us many things and He connected us with Shabd Naam. And all the passions—lust, anger, greed, etc.—He made it possible for us to remove them; in fact, He helped us in removing all these passions. And after making us perfect, He gave us the limitless wealth of Naam, which we are using. Moreover, to those who are coming to us, we are giving them the wealth also. But all we have done, and all that we have, that is all because of our Master, Guru Ramdas; that is why, millions of times we are sacrificing ourselves on Him.

Hazur Maharaj Kirpal used to say, "If you love me, practice my teachings and obey my commandments." All the Perfect Masters—those Who have come in the past and those Who will come in the future—have never up until now allowed us to do any bad things, and They have emphasized the necessity of keeping ourselves pure. They say that the purer you keep your heart, the more you will progress in meditation and the more you will go above.

He is not an ascetic who is greedy in his heart
and every day wanders about for the sake
of Maya.
First he was called with respect but he did
not come to take the alms.
Later on he repented and made his son sit
among the others.
All the righteous people started laughing when
the ascetic was swayed in the wave of greed.
Where the ascetic sees little wealth he does
not go near, but where he sees a lot he
loses his religion.
O brother, he is not an ascetic - he is a crane:
Thus think the Sadhus.
The ascetic criticizes the Sat Purush and is
praised in the world - and for this fault
he is killed by God.
Look at what fruit the yogi got by criticizing
the great souls: He lost all he had earned.
Outside he sits among the righteous people
and is called an "ascetic", but when he
sits inside he commits sins.
The Lord shows his inner sins to the righteous
people.
The Lord of Judgment says to the angels of
Yama, "Seize this yogi and put him in
the place where the great murderers are!"

No one should have any connection with this ascetic again as he is rejected by the Satguru.
Nanak has told what is happening at the court of the Lord. He who understands it will improve his life.
The devotees of the Lord meditate on the Lord and this is the greatness of the Lord.
The devotees of the Lord sing the praises of the Lord always.
The Naam of the Lord is the happiness giver.
The devotees of the Lord are always blessed with the Glory of Naam, which increases every day.
The devotees of the Lord are made to sit in an immovable house and the Lord Himself preserves their honor.
The Lord will ask for the account of the critics and will punish them severely.
Whatever the critics have earned in their heart, they will get that fruit accordingly.
Whatever is done in the heart will manifest outside even if it is done sitting within the earth.
Nanak says, I have become happy seeing the Glory of the Lord.
The Lord Himself is the Protector of the devotees.
What can the sinner do against them?

The foolish egotist practiced egoism and
dies eating poison.
As a ripe field is harvested, few are the days
of life.
Their reward will be as the deeds they have
done.
The Lord of humble Nanak is great - he is
the Lord of all.

14

The Crushing of the Ego

He is not an ascetic who is greedy in his heart and everyday wanders about for the sake of Maya.

This is the bani of Sri Guru Ramdas Ji Maharaj. Those who have been attending Satsang at the Sant Bani Ashram are very familiar with this bani of Guru Ramdas, on which I have been giving Satsang for the last two weeks. They might remember that in the beginning Guru Ramdas talked about the ascetic or yogi who was opposing his Master. So now he says, Who is the real ascetic? Who is the real yogi? He who is free of pride, jealousy, egoism, and negative habits. In the Path of the Masters, showing miracles and using supernatural powers is not allowed; those powers are of no importance. In the Path of the Masters, Saints and Mahatmas tell us how to meditate on Shabd Naam—because our soul has come into this world to meditate on Shabd Naam and go back to our Home.

So lovingly He tells us that if we have love and yearning for God, if we want to realize Him, and if we have longing to meet Him, then we should abstain from these bad habits. Lust, anger, greed, attachment and egoism: all these are retarding factors, and we should always abstain from them. Out of these, greed is a very dangerous passion, and if we want to realize God we should become free from this bad habit of greed.

First he was called with respect but he did not come to take the alms.
Later on he repented and made his son sit among the others.

You know that that yogi used to oppose the Master, Guru Amardas, very much. So here, Guru Ramdas Ji is telling us the story of what happened to him. Because he was opposing and criticizing, and because the Masters are always gracious and They always try Their best to forgive Their critics, Guru Amardas invited him to eat with Him. But the yogi was so much against Guru Amardas Ji that He wouldn't accept the invitation. He said, "What is the use of going to such a person?"

Later on, Guru Amardas Ji announced that anyone who ate in the langar, would not only be fed free, but they would be given a lot of wealth. When this was announced, many people came to eat the food, including that ascetic—but he didn't dare to come all the way in and eat the food with the other dear ones. He was interested, though; and he was walking here and there outside the langar, thinking that maybe Guru Amardas would come out and invite him again, and this time he would accept. But Guru Amardas didn't come out; he had invited him already, but he hadn't come; what was the use of inviting him again? Guru Amardas knew that he was waiting outside, but he paid no attention to him. Anyway nobody came to invite him, and he didn't dare come in, but he was attracted by the wealth, so he thought of sending his son. So he sent his son in his place to eat and collect the promised wealth, but when the Satsangis and others who knew the story saw his son, they laughed at him and said, "Look at that yogi! How greedy he is! He was criticizing Guru Amardas on the grounds that he was greedy for name and fame and wealth; now he cannot control his greed, so he sends his son to take the wealth!" Greed is such a funny thing.

So here in the bani, Guru Ramdas says, "Greed makes us criticize others." Master Kirpal Singh used to say that those who find fault with others have some self-interest behind that. Nobody criticizes anyone without self-interest.

In India, the householders invite those people who leave their homes and go in the wilderness and become so-called "sadhus" to have food and visit with them, and they think that they are doing a good deed and will get the blessings of God. In the olden days, when these "sadhus" used to go to people's houses to eat food, the householders would make very delicious food for them because they wanted to please God. And after eating the food, the sadhus would ask for money to cover the wear and tear of their teeth. They would say, "We ate your food using our teeth, and you should pay us for that." So the householders also gave them money.

When I was searching for God in my youth, once I was in the company of one Lundu Baba, a so-called "sadhu," and we were going from one place to another in search of God. Once when we were in Punjab, we came to a farmer's home and he prepared very delicious food for us. After eating the food, that Baba asked for that wear and tear money. The farmer gave one rupee to me and another rupee to the Baba. I did not want the money and I gave it to the Baba, but the farmer felt very bad. He said, "If this is going to happen, my religious deed will not be completed. Unless you accept the money, I won't get any benefit." I told him lovingly, "Listen, I am not after money. I am the son of a farmer, I have even more wealth than you have. And I can eat any food, I don't have to eat all this good food. But I am in search of God, and that is why I am accompanying this Baba. And I don't accept any money because I have a lot of my own, so I am giving this money to him." So that Baba took the money quietly and put it in his pocket without saying anything. I told that farmer, "Up until now I have eaten many types of different food, very hard food and very soft food also, but I have never found that my teeth suffered any wear and tear; I still have good teeth."

The point is this: The so-called "sadhus" go to people's houses and eat food, and even then because they are so greedy, they ask for the "wear and tear" money. They find some excuse for getting money from the householders. And because the so-called "sadhus" are tempted by wealth, Guru Amardas Ji invited that ascetic for lunch and when he didn't come, in order to tempt him, he announced that he would give away a lot of money. And because the yogi couldn't control his greed, yet didn't dare go himself, he sent his son.

I was born in a Sikh family and I had the idea that if you visit the holy places where the great Masters have been, you can get liberation and peace of mind. So I left no place out; I visited every place where the past Masters had gone—all the holy places, all the great temples—but I didn't get any peace. And when I came to Baba Bishan Das, he told me that unless we go within, unless we visit the most holy place that is the human body, we cannot realize God. Baba Bishan Das told me that unless we go within, we cannot get rid of greed and other passions. He told me that the waves of greed, lust, anger, all come from within. Nothing comes from outside. Outside, we just act according to the feelings or thoughts which have come in our mind. Since the disease comes from within, then the medicine for removing the disease is also within.

All the righteous people started laughing when the ascetic was swayed in the wave of greed.
Where the ascetic sees little wealth he does not go near, but where he sees a lot he loses his religion.
O brother, he is not an ascetic—he is a crane: Thus think the Sadhus.

> **The ascetic criticizes the Sat Purush and is praised in the world—and for this fault he is killed by God.**
> **Look at what fruit the yogi got by criticizing the great souls: He lost all he had earned.**
> **Outside he sits among the righteous people and is called an "ascetic," but when he sits inside he commits sins.**
> **The Lord shows his inner sins to the righteous people.**
> **The Lord of Judgment says to the angels of Yama, "Seize this yogi and put him in the place where the great murderers are!"**

We can deceive the world, but we cannot deceive God, because he is sitting within us and watching our every single action. Guru Sahib says that he is not an ascetic who is envious, jealous and critical of others. He is a false devotee, a false worshiper of God; he is like a crane who stands in the water pretending he is doing the devotion; he is standing on one leg and closing his eyes as if he were doing the devotion of the Lord. But in his mind he is only thinking of catching fish. And whenever he gets any opportunity he catches a fish and eats it. He who is critical and jealous of others is not a *tapa* or ascetic. Never think that nobody is seeing the karma; God is seeing everything. Even if you sit for meditation in the world below, still you will be manifested outside; the fragrance of your meditation will be spread all over, in the sky, on the earth, everywhere. The devotee of the Lord who meditates on the Naam of the Lord twenty-four hours a day, doesn't remain hidden.

In the same way, if we go underground and commit any sin, the bad smell of that deed will spread all over, and God will know it. So here he says, when the end time of that yogi came, God ordered the Lord of Judgment to send that tapa to such a place where the great sinners were gathered. We know that if we are aware of whatever law we live under, but don't obey it, then we are likely to get more punishment than those who don't know anything about the law. In the same way, if we are called "Mahatmas" or "devotees" or "great meditators" and many people worship us, and then if we are not really great meditators and Mahatmas and are doing bad deeds, we will get much more punishment—millions of times more punishment—than ordinary people.

Kabir Sahib says that those who teach others but don't practice what they teach will get sand in their mouths. And those people who take care of other people's courtyards, but don't protect their own field, they will always repent. First of all one should have control of his own mind; then he might try to teach others. First of all we should extinguish our own fire, and then we might be able to extinguish other people's fires. But what is our condition? We are burning with the fire of lust, anger, greed, attachment, and egoism, and we are planning and scheming to save other people from this fire.

So when the Lord of Judgment was told by God to send that tapa to the place where the great sinners were, then the Lord of Judgment told his angels, his servants, "You send him to such a place where nobody can see him, because he has criticized the Sat Purush."

No one should have any connection with this ascetic again as he is rejected by the Satguru.
Nanak has told what is happening at the court of the Lord. He who understands it will improve his life.

Guru Ramdas Ji says, "Don't think that I have made up this story to frighten you. I am telling you exactly what is happening in the Court of the Lord, and how critics and criminals are getting punished. If you don't believe it, meditate and go within and see how God is punishing those who are pretending to be Mahatmas but are not, and those who are teaching others and not practicing themselves. Go within and see."

Often I say that in order to recognize a Master, you must look at his life history and see whether he has done any meditation in his life, whether he has spent years in deep meditation.

The devotees of the Lord meditate on the Lord and this is the greatness of the Lord.
The devotees of the Lord sing the praises of the Lord always.
The Naam of the Lord is the happiness giver.

The Beloveds of God, the Great Souls come from the Eternal Home, and are already Saints; and as soon as they come in contact with a Perfect Master, their veil is removed. They come prepared, but in order to demonstrate to us that we cannot achieve anything without work, they work day and night, meditate a lot, and make their lives pure, just to show us that we also cannot achieve anything unless we work hard.

Dadu Sahib says, "Dadu talks about God Whom he has seen with his own eyes, while others talk about God Whom they have heard about or read about in books." Further He says that the Vedas or other holy books do not convince us of the existence of God, because they only *tell* us that God exists. They cannot really convince us. People don't like to meditate; they want to get convinced by reading the books. But it is not possible. He says that there is butter in the milk but unless we churn it, we cannot get it; we won't be convinced that the butter is there until we churn it.

The devotees of the Lord are always blessed with the Glory of Naam, which increases every day.
The devotees of the Lord are made to sit in an immovable house and the Lord Himself preserves their honor.
The Lord will ask for the account of the critics and will punish them severely.
Whatever the critics have earned in their heart, they will get that fruit accordingly.
Whatever is done in the heart will manifest outside even if it is done sitting within the earth.
Nanak says, "I have become happy seeing the Glory of the Lord."

The Beloveds of God are as dear to God as brothers are dear to sisters, and children to their mother. And those who do the devotion of the Lord, and become His beloveds, God opens His door for them, and when they enter the Court of the Lord, they are honored. The account of the critic will be seen, and he will have to explain to God why he did that. We may sit inside and create karma thinking that nobody else is seeing, but inevitably we have to suffer or enjoy the reaction of that.

He says, "When I met God and saw His justice, I realized that whatever one is doing, he is suffering or enjoying the reactions of his deeds." Guru Nanak says, "After creating the entire universe, the Lord has kept one accountant who keeps the account of all the souls. At that place only the true ones are accepted; the false ones are rejected."

The Lord Himself is the Protector of the devotees.
What can the sinner do against them?

Since God is the Protector of His beloveds, since He is taking care of His children, what can the sinners do? They can only go on doing sins and increasing their burden.

King Hirnaikash had many boons from the Negative Power: He could not be killed by either human or animal, he could not die in the daytime or nighttime, and he could not die either indoors or outdoors. With these boons he became full of ego and thought, "I am never going to die! There is no time when it is neither day nor night; there is nobody who is neither man nor animal, and there is no place that is neither inside nor outside; I am not going to die. So why shouldn't I make people do my devotion, as though I were God?" He started telling everybody, "Repeat this: In the water there is Hirnaikash, on the earth there is Hirnaikash, in the past Hirnaikash was God, and in the future also Hirnaikash will be God." He made everybody do his devotion, and God did not like that, so He sent a pure soul, whose name was Prahlad, who was born as his son. When Prahlad started going to school, he was taught that mantra: "Hirnaikash is the only God: he was in the past, he will be in the future, he is in the water, he is everywhere," etc., etc. But Prahlad didn't like that, because he was a real devotee of God, and he said, "No, this is not true. On the land there is God, in the water there is God, in the past God was God, and in the future also God will be God."

So the teacher was unhappy because he was under the orders of Hirnaikash, so he went to Hirnaikash and said, "Oh Lord, your son is a spoiled child; he is not obeying what I tell him. Not only is he spoiled, but he is spoiling other children also, because he is saying, 'Hirnaikash is not God, but God is God!' He is not doing your devotion." So Hirnaikash called for Prahlad, and when he came he asked him why he was not doing his devotion. Prahlad was a true soul sent by God to crush Hirnaikash in his egoism. So he replied, "Why should I believe in you? One day you are going to die. I must do the devotion of the Lord Who is immortal, Who is not involved in birth and death, and Who will liberate me. That is why I am remembering His Name and not yours."

Hearing this, Hirnaikash became so angry that he took out his sword to kill Prahlad right then. But he couldn't do it. After that, he tried many times to kill Prahlad. Once he threw him from the top of a mountain, but still Prahlad was saved; God always protects His devotees.

Finally, when nothing was successful in killing Prahlad, Hirnaikash made a metal pillar and heated it, and told Prahlad, "Now I will see if the Lord you believe in exists. I will see how He is going to save you from this heated pillar. Now embrace this!" Prahlad was a real devotee and that is why he had *full faith in God,* and that no matter what happened he would always be protected, and he said, "Yes, I have been saying this in the past, and I say it again: the Lord exists; you are not He; there is an ultimate Lord and I am doing His devotion. He has been protecting me before, and he will protect me now."

Happily, and without any hesitation, he embraced that heated pillar and it became cool and burst asunder; and out of it stepped God incarnated as Narsing—half-man, half-lion—and as it was twilight—neither complete night nor complete day—Narsing caught Hirnaikash in the doorway so that he was neither completely outside nor completely inside, and tore him apart.

So Guru Nanak Sahib says, "God doesn't like people to have ego. Egos are crushed by God." God has created his devotees in all four ages, and He has been saving their honor and protecting them in all four ages. He saved Prahlad and He killed Hirnaikash. He has always defeated the egoistic people and saved and protected His devotees.

> **The foolish egotist practiced egoism and dies eating poison.**
> **As a ripe field is harvested, few are the days of life.**
> **Their reward will be as the deeds they have done.**
> **The Lord of humble Nanak is great—He is the Lord of all.**

We should do the devotion of the Lord to make our lives successful. The human body which we have been given is a precious opportunity in which we can meet God and do His devotion. Out of the eighty-four lakhs creatures, God has made the human being superior; He has made him the leader of all creation. And those who misuse this opportunity of the human body will come and go in the different lower forms of creatures; and they will suffer.